D1240056

IT CAME OUT FIGHTING!

Cadillac Motor Car Division's rise to dominance of the luxury car market after World War II

Jeffrey D. Shively

authorHOUSE®

AuthorHouse™
1663 Liberty Drive, Suite 200
Bloomington, IN 47403 www.authorhouse.com
Phone: 1-800-839-8640

First published by AuthorHouse 8/6/2008

ISBN: 978-1-4343-4834-0 (sc)

Printed in the United States of America
Bloomington, Indiana
This book is printed on acid-free paper.

Contents

Introduction

The most profound historical questions sometimes arise from the humblest of sources. In 1989, I purchased my first car, an Alpine Turquoise 1965 Cadillac Sedan deVille. I knew that this would be a fine machine, because Cadillac had a grand reputation for quality. I already had a love of history, so I began researching my car at the school library. My research turned up very little, but my findings were enough to whet my appetite. Over 181,000 new car buyers chose to spend their hard earned money on new Cadillacs during the 1965 model year, more than any other luxury marque.[1] There had to be a reason for this.

There were alternatives within the fine car field. Packard had perished in 1958, but Lincoln and Imperial were still going strong. Mercedes-Benz and Rolls-Royce exported cars to the United States as well. Lincoln produced little more than 40,000 units during the 1965 model year. The cars were slightly heavier than the Cadillacs, and were considerably more expensive, with a base price ten percent higher than its rival.[2] That factor might have contributed for the lower sales at Lincoln, but more was in play. Chrysler's luxury entry, Imperial, fared even worse, selling only 18,000 cars.[3] Despite the best efforts of other luxury makes, Cadillac outsold its domestic rivals by a three to one ratio. Including foreign entries, the ratio dropped only to two to one. Observers of the day noted that the 1965 Cadillac was superior mechanically and stylistically to the competition. These cars are still favored by collectors four decades after they left the factory because of their legendary reliability. Even *Motor Trend*, which in the 1965 model year still permitted its writers to praise domestic cars, noted that the new Cadillac was in the same league as foreign cars costing over $15,000.[4]

The question of Cadillac's dominance of the luxury field continued to percolate though my undergraduate years. I began collecting in earnest after college, at one point having nine Cadillacs in my care. I became familiar with the pre-war years, thanks to my ownership of a 1941 Series 62 deluxe coupe and a 1942 Series 62 sedan. They were built to the same high standards as my first car had been. It seemed that the question that I raised at age sixteen had deeper roots than I had originally supposed. Perhaps the answer would be found in the early 1940s.

In late 2004, a possible solution to my query about Cadillac's dominance presented itself from an unlikely source. I needed a new engine for my '41. I was offered a low mileage unit by a fellow collector. There were only one catch. It had been produced by Cadillac during World War II as a tank engine. I did some research and found that it would work in my car. Many internal parts were changed for improved durability under wartime conditions, so I was getting a better engine than the original unit. On the drive back from South Carolina, it occurred to me that perhaps the answer to my long held question of Cadillac's dominance was sitting upside down in the bed of my rented truck. It seemed entirely possible that Cadillac's wartime activities might have held the key to its postwar success. An investigation was in order. What follows is a product of that research.

Cadillac's dominance of the luxury car field took hold in earnest after the Second World War. The transition to mastery began several years before America's entry into the war, but Cadillac's wartime production of engines and automatic transmissions allowed the company to come out of the war far more prepared than its rivals to resume peacetime pursuits. Coupled with an advertising campaign that consistently portrayed Cadillac as the definitive luxury car, the company was able to forge a grip over the luxury car market that took fifty years and clever accounting tactics to overcome.[5]

Automotive production ground to a halt in the fabled Clark Avenue plant on February 5, 1942.[6] Two months later, the first Cadillac built M-5 tank rolled down the assembly line. At the same time, internal parts for the Allison V-1710 liquid cooled aircraft engine were being stamped, cast, and machined in this legendary plant. Before the war ended, the M-8 motorized howitzer and M-24 tank were also rumbling out of Clark Avenue and onto railcars bound for the coasts. Many factors contributed to Cadillac's rise to dominance, some of them occurring decades before the outbreak of hostilities. Cadillac's founder, Henry M. Leland, learned the value of precision manufacturing during the Civil War. He applied those principles to auto production much earlier than his competitors. Cadillac has always been a leader in technological advancement, from the self starter of the 1910s to the Northstar System of the 2000s.[7] Precision manufacturing and constant innovation increased reliability of the cars while lowering the cost per unit. General Motors' sales and marketing staff positioned Cadillac as the most prestigious car in the company's lineup. Buyers of G.M. products were directed from Chevrolet through the mid-priced brands, and eventually into a Cadillac showroom.[8] Packard, Pierce-Arrow, Marmon, and other luxury makes did not have this advantage.

Cadillac changed the meaning of luxury with the introduction of a personal luxury car, the 1938 Series 60 Special. No longer was a luxury car something only to be driven by the chauffer. The owner could now participate fully in the experience, as the driver of his own fine automobile. For the next several decades, Cadillac was able to define itself as the standard in the fine car field thanks to high quality and an aggressive advertising program. In the last full year of production before America's entry into World War II, Cadillac produced the world's first truly modern luxury car. With this as the last memory of the company before the war, many buyers were likely in a mindset to purchase a Cadillac after peace returned.

The importance of wartime production can not be overlooked. It could even be said that Cadillac's military production was the linchpin that secured that company's postwar dominance. Cadillac found after World War I that soldiers who had driven these cars during the war were more likely to buy them after returning home.[9] This lesson was likely not lost a generation later.

By training thousands of mechanics skilled at working on Cadillac military engines, the company insured a ready supply of "Cadillac Servicemen" to fill postwar garages. In combat during World War II, tank crews undoubtedly appreciated the reliability of their machines, as poorly functioning equipment was a death sentence on the battlefield. It is very reasonable to suspect that when these veterans returned to their offices and boardrooms in 1946, they would be prime candidates to buy new Cadillacs.

Image was as important to Cadillac as the quality of its machines. The ruggedness and reliability of the military engine was touted in wartime Cadillac ads. Production of internal parts for the legendary Allison V-1710 aircraft engine allowed Cadillac to showcase precision engineering while tapping into the romance of aviation, themes that would be used by the marque well into the 1990s.[10]

The success of conversion at Cadillac Motor Car Division in 1941-1942 and reconversion forty months later tremendously impacted the company's post war fortunes. Competitors like Packard and Lincoln were at a serious disadvantage during the opening months of the 1946 model year because they had produced non-automotive goods during the war. Reconversion required removing all of the military tooling from the plants and re-installing these companies' automotive tooling, a very costly proposition. By contrast, Cadillac spent the duration perfecting an already outstanding drive train combination, allowing it to give the luxury car buyer a product that was more than a warmed over 1942 model. Prior to World War II, Packard typically out-produced Cadillac in absolute numbers. This happened a few times after the war, but at terrible cost to Packard.[11] Tank production helped Cadillac complete the transition to the ruler of the luxury car field during the post war era. By 1950,the company was the undisputed king of the fine car market, a position that it would not relinquish until the turn of the 21st century.

Introduction Notes

1   Mary Sieber and Ken Buttolph, eds., *Standard Catalog of Cadillac: 1903-1990* (Iola, Wisconsin: Krause Publications, 1991),244-245.

2   John Gunnell, ed., *Standard Catalog of American Cars: 1946-1975* (Iola, Wisconsin: Krause Publications, 1991), 426.

3   Ibid., 248.

4   John Ethridge, "GM's Crown Jewel," *Motor Trend,* August 1965, 38.

5   2000 BMW Production Figures; available from http://64224.175.31/european_companies/BMW/bmwsales.htm; accessed 30 May, 2005.

   2000 Cadillac Production Figures; available from http://64.224.175.31/nao_companies/general_motors/gmsales3htm; accessed 30 May, 2005.

   2000 Lexus Production Figures; available from http://64.224.175.31/asian_companies/toyota_motor/business/toyota-us-sales-2000-by-model.htm; accessed 30 May, 2005.

   2000 Mercedes Benz Production Figures; available from http://64.224.175.31/nao_companies/daimlerchrysler/dc-business-figures/merc-pass-car-sales-01.htm; accessed 30 May, 2005.

6   Roy A. Schneider, *Cadillacs of the Forties* (Temple City, California: Cadillac Motorbooks, 1999), 77.

7   Cadillac Motor Car Division, *Seville 2000*(General Motors Corporation, Detroit, Michigan, 2000), 24.

8   Juliann Sivulka, *Soap, Sex, and Cigarettes: A Cultural History of American Advertising* (Wadsworth Publishing Agency: Belmont, CA, 1998), 177.

9   Cadillac Motor Car Division, *Cadillac Participation in the World War* (Detroit, MI: Cadillac Motor Car Company, 1919), 11, 19-21.

10   Cadillac Motor Car Division, *2002 Seville (*Detroit, Michigan: General Motors Corporation, 2001), 13.

11   Gunnell, 522-24.Sieber and Buttolph, 231.

Part I

Cadillac Before World War II

Cadillac was not pre-ordained to be the mark by which all other cars would be judged. A great deal of vision and hard work went into producing a motorcar that was not only good enough to survive the cut-throat competition of the brass era, but has been able to carry on for over a century. Innovation was the key to Cadillac's early success. Beginning with interchangeable parts, progressing through the days of the early V-8 and self starter, to the introduction of the first V-16, engineering excellence was Cadillac's calling card. The seeds of post-war dominance trace their roots back to the Civil War. Without Henry Leland's guiding hand, it is likely that Cadillac would have gone the way of hundreds of other manufacturers.

Chapter 1

Mr. Leland's Dream
1861-1915

The story of Cadillac begins in a Barton, Vermont, farm house. On February 16, 1843, Henry Martyn Leland was born to Leander and Zylpha Leland.[12] Young Mr. Leland learned the value of hard work on that farm. When war came to the nation in 1861, he yearned to join his elder brother in service of the Union, but was too young for service. Instead, Mr. Leland contributed to the war effort by laboring as a machinist at the Crompton Works in Worchester, Massachusetts, producing gun stocks. After the war, he joined Colt Revolver in Hartford, Connecticut. There he learned the importance of precision machining and interchangeable parts.[13] Easily repaired firearms meant the difference between victory and defeat on the battlefield. He realized the implications for industry as a whole. If all manufactured goods could be produced from a standardized pool of parts, the price per unit would fall and reliability would rise.

The United States during the decades following the Civil War was a nation that was finally experiencing the full effect of the Industrial Revolution. The demand for precisely machined products grew accordingly. One of Mr. Leland's first successes in selling the idea of precision was with the Westinghouse Air Brake Company in 1880. Air brakes were state of the art technology at that time in the railroad industry. Early applications were disappointing, as the brake cylinders and pistons were so crudely machined that they leaked air, resulting in poor stopping. Mr. Leland's employer, Brown and Sharpe, produced a new lathe that corrected the problem and allowed the brakes to function as intended.[14] Henry Leland soon understood that the relentless pursuit of precision required a company of his own to be fully realized.

Mr. Leland moved west in 1890, settling in Detroit. The city was home to a variety of industries, from ship building and marine engines, to tools used by the Michigan timber industry. Despite the high level of industrial activities, there were only nine machine shops in the city as late as 1890. On September 19 of that year, Leland, Faulconer and Norton was incorporated. As the vice-president and general manager, it was Mr. Leland's job to scour the upper-Midwest for contracts.[15] During the first three years of operation, the firm produced such varied products as typesetters, typewriters, repeating rifles, Motorcycles, and milk condensers. Leland, Faulconer and Norton became Leland and Falconer in 1894 when Mr. Norton moved back east to spend time with his family.[16]

The firm grew tremendously during the 1890s. In 1896, Leland and Faulconer erected a state of the art foundry. Henry Leland often personally tested the castings produced here, discovering that nearly half did not meet his rigid standard for quality. This distressed Robert Faulconer, who was concerned primarily with cost.[17] Mr. Leland's response to this objection was typical of the man.

> There always was and there always will be a conflict between Good and Good Enough, and in opening up a new business or new department one can count upon meeting this resistance to a high standard of workmanship. It is easy to get cooperation for mediocre work, but one must sweat blood for a chance to produce a superior product.[18]

This insistence on quality would be carried over to his days at Cadillac Motor Car Company, a tradition adhered to for generations after Mr. Leland's passing.

The bicycle craze of the 1890s demanded that manufacturers produce quality gears for cyclists. Leland and Faulconer obliged, producing gears for a myriad of companies, including the George N. Pierce Company of Buffalo, New York. Eventually, this firm would produce the fabled Pierce-Arrow motorcar from 1901 to 1938. In 1896, Leland and Faulconer built its first gasoline engine. Three years later, car manufacturer Ransom E. Olds, was in need of a quiet and efficient transmission. Mr. Olds promptly signed Leland's firm to build the transmissions. These were an immediate hit with Olds employees, who were impressed with the precision and interchangeability of the units.

Customers appreciated the quiet and reliable shifting and began buying Oldsmobiles as fast as the Lansing, Michigan factory could produce them.[19] Tragedy befell Olds on March 9, 1901, when a fire destroyed the engine department of the factory. Henry Leland immediately signed a contract to produce 2,000 engines for Olds, an unprecedented number for one year's production. Dodge Brothers, Inc. also produced engines for Olds during this crisis. Despite building engines of identical designs, the Leland and Faulconer engine produced nearly a quarter more horsepower than the Dodge version.[20] Mr. Leland's insistence on precision made all the difference.

The Detroit Automobile Company was organized in 1899 under the direction of chief engineer Henry Ford. The firm collapsed a year later, a victim of Mr. Ford's preoccupation with building race machines, rather than focusing on more practical and profitable passenger automobiles. In late 1901, the company was revived as the Henry Ford Company. Mr. Ford soon left, and the situation became dire. Henry Leland knew that the company could be salvaged and then used as a basis for bringing precision engineering to all phases of automobile manufacture. On August 22, 1902, the Henry Ford Company was reorganized under Henry Leland's leadership as Cadillac Automobile Company, taking its name from the French explorer who had first set foot upon the ground that is present day Detroit two centuries earlier. The first automobile to bear the

Cadillac name was a simple one-cylinder runabout completed on October 17, 1902.[21] The car was the hit of the Third Annual National Automobile Show, held at Madison Square Garden on January 17-24, 1903. Orders for 2,286 units, more than the planned 1903 production, were processed within a few weeks. A legend was born.

Cadillac's product line grew from a single runabout to touring cars and enclosed doctor's coupes by 1908. That year, the company coined the slogan, "Standard of the World." This claim was not simple boastfulness. In 1904, Englishman Sir Thomas Dewar initiated a competition for the most significant advance in automotive technology during the previous year. Fredrick S. Bennett, the legendary importer of American automobiles into Great Britain, was particularly fond of Cadillac. So impressed was he with the quality of Cadillac that he convinced the Royal Automobile Club to oversee a test of interchangeability. Three identical, factory fresh 1908 Cadillacs were selected from the Anglo-American Motor Car Company's recent shipment on a London dock. During the period of March 2-4, 1908, the cars were disassembled and their parts mixed together with spares from the company store. All three machines were then reassembled from the jumble of parts. True interchangeability would be unknown in the British car industry for several decades to come. Much to the consternation of the stuffy Brits, the cars started and ran perfectly at the Brooklands Motordrome for 500 miles, averaging thirty four miles per hour. To further prove the superiority of the Cadillac to other automobiles, one of the three cars was then run in the Royal Automobile Club's "2000 Mile Trial" in June 1908, winning its class. There was little disagreement when the 1909 Dewar Trophy was awarded to Cadillac in February of that year.[22]

Cadillac, the innovator

Innovations at Cadillac did not end when the company was acquired by William C. Durant as part of General Motors on July 29, 1909 for $4,500,000.[23] The 1912 Cadillac was the first production automobile to have an electric lighting system. No longer did drivers have to ignite dangerous acetylene gas to drive at night. Charles Kettering of Dayton Engineering Laboratories spearheaded the development of a truly automatic electric self starter. Thousands of motorists were injured or killed annually when backfiring engines spun their cranks in the hands of the unfortunate drivers, breaking their wrists or worse. The self starter required no such efforts and provided for safe starting under all conditions. The company's foresight was rewarded with another Dewar Trophy in 1913.[24]

Cadillac had advanced from being a single cylinder car to four cylinder motivation by 1909. The four cylinder was even more reliable than its predecessor. The "Type 30" served until 1914. The following year, Cadillac scored yet another coup with the introduction of the first V-type eight cylinder engine. The cylinder banks met the crankcase at a ninety degree angle, an arrangement that most V-8s follow to the present day. The new engine was balanced and powerful, generating seventy horsepower. Other luxury makes were caught by surprise. Packard was still using a large inline six cylinder engine at the time. The January 2, 1915 issue of the *Saturday Evening Post* featured what has become the most famous Cadillac ad of all time, "The Penalty of Leadership."[25] The text noted the challenges of being a leader in a given field, as the leader was always the target of lesser and envious people. Cadillac, although an adolescent, was the technological leader in the automotive industry in 1915.

Chapter 1 Notes

[12] Winifred C. Leland, *Master of Precision: Henry M. Leland* (Detroit, Michigan: Wayne State University Press, 1966), 19-21.

[13] Ibid., 24-30.

[14] Ibid., 47-50.

[15] Ibid., 52-53.

[16] Ibid., 56.

[17] Ibid., 58-59.

[18] Ibid., 59.

[19] Ibid., 60-61.

[20] Ibid., 61-63.

[21] Walter M.P. McCall, *Eighty Years of Cadillac LaSalle* (Osceola, Wisconsin: Motorbooks International Publishers, 1982), 6.

[22] Ibid., 30.

[23] Arthur Pound, *The turning wheel; the story of General Motors through twenty-five years, 1908-1933* (Garden City, New York: Doubleday, Doran and Company, inc., 1934), 109.

[24] McCall, 46.

[25] Sivulka,114.

Chapter 2

Cadillac in war and peace 1917-1929

The United States entered World War I in April 1917 ill-prepared for fighting a global war. It was clear that this war would be mechanized to a greater degree than any yet fought. Officers needed reliable transportation at the battlefront, so the United States Army began its search for a staff car. Some Allied nations were using older Cadillacs on the battlefield with great success.[26] The U.S. Army had used a small number of Cadillacs during Mexican skirmishes during recent years. Although it seemed logical that the War Department would choose Cadillac to fill its wartime needs, the government had to make it official.

Staff cars and balloon wenches for the Army

In July 1917, the U.S. Army staged a test in Marfa, Texas to select its new staff car. There were no paved roads upon which the cars could travel, only the sun baked desert floor. The test was intended to cover 2,000 miles, but the Cadillac traveled an additional 3,000 for good measure. During the test, the car averaged twelve miles per gallon and used only one and a half gallons of water, remarkable statistics for that era. The U.S. Army promptly selected the Cadillac as the standard seven passenger car for its European operations.[27]

The 1917 Cadillac touring cars needed few modifications for their new roles. An extra gasoline tank was mounted on the running board and each vehicle was equipped with chains for pulling itself out of the mire. Little else other than an olive drab paint job differentiated military cars from the rest of Cadillac production. Only 199 of the 2,294 open touring cars built for the U.S. Army remained Stateside. An additional 300 enclosed seven passenger limousines were outfitted similarly and shipped to Europe.[28] Cadillac's 7,000 employees easily integrated this additional production into the assembly line.[29]

The seven passenger Cadillac touring cars were immediately welcomed by American forces in Europe. General Pershing's personal car was a Cadillac, something which he undoubtedly relished. Other officers most certainly thought as highly of their cars as their commander. Although there was little time for regular maintenance, the Cadillacs performed exceptionally well. Many spent as much as three weeks at the front with no mechanical difficulty.[30] Some of the glowing words from drivers in Europe included the following.

> The weak and unworthy were weeded out, and the strong and capable were thrust prominently forward to shoulder new and heavy affairs, which taxed ability, resourcefulness, and endurance.[31]

Another serviceman claimed that, "Men who used Cadillac cars in France actually speak of them as staunch pals."[32] Still another stated:

> It was my privilege to have for my service a Cadillac for one particular twelve thousand mile trip and during the time there was never a single interruption from anything except tire trouble.[33]

The record of Cadillac on the battlefield was impeccable. Existing records do not show how many servicemen bought Cadillacs after the war because of their experiences, but it is fair to assume that more than a few veterans chose not to buy a Packard or Pierce Arrow because of the reliability exhibited by Cadillac during World War I.

Cadillac's activities during World War I were not confined to automobile production. Henry Leland wanted to build Liberty aircraft engines at Cadillac to help the war effort, but met with resistance from General Motors founder William C. Durant. Mr. Leland left his own company in July 1917 to produce these engines. He named his new corporation after a hero of his youth, and the first man for whom he voted, Abraham Lincoln.[34] This new company was soon producing seventy aircraft engines per day at the Lincoln plant on Holden Avenue in Detroit.[35] Not long after Mr. Leland's departure, Durant changed his mind on aircraft engine production. More than 30,000 Liberty engines were produced over the next few years. Cadillac engineers helped improve the engine by using Mr. Leland's principles of precision, eventually solving an oiling problem by introducing a pressure feeding system in 1918.[36] Aircraft engines were useless without well trained mechanics to service them. The Cadillac Technical School was converted to the Liberty Engine School in 1918 to train these technicians.[37]

Cadillac produced other items for the military. A two-ton artillery tractor was powered by a Cadillac engine with an improved oil pump with two oil sumps to insure proper oiling when the crawler-tracked machine traversed uneven terrain that it would not suffer from oil starvation. Some Cadillac chassis were modified to carry a searchlight. This beast weighed nearly 8,000 pounds.[38] The sixty inch lens pierced the night in search of nocturnal intruders.

Despite the great weight of the vehicle, it had a top speed of over fifty miles per hour.[39] Perhaps the most interesting application was a balloon winch powered by a Cadillac engine. The wench was used to maintain observation balloons at a proper height for spotting enemy troop movements and to quickly draw them safely back to earth in case of attack.[40] The war had been good for Cadillac, allowing it to continue producing cars while landing lucrative government contracts.

Cadillac in the Roaring '20s

Cadillac continued to innovate during the 1920s. The company moved to a new factory complex on Clark Avenue, Detroit, in 1921. At the time of the move, five of the eight planned buildings were already completed. This new plant would produce Cadillacs for the next seventy years.[41] In 1927,the LaSalle was launched. This new car was the first American production automobile to be styled professionally. Previously, functionality had been the primary concern for manufacturers. The LaSalle was a luxury car in quality but not in price, something new to the industry.[42] Two years later, Cadillac introduced the Syncho-Mesh Silent-Shift, the world's first synchronized transmission.[43] Double-clutching and grinding gears were now a thing of the past, replaced by a smoothly shifting transmission. Thermo-control of water-cooling system was introduced in 1925, as was crankcase ventilation, followed by silent poppet valve mechanisms in 1930.[44] These innovations, although now highly evolved, are still found on the modern automobile.

Introducing new technology is pointless for a company if there is no reason for consumers to buy a new product. By the 1920s, General Motors was producing cars whose quality was second to none. The public seemed to agree as sales rose from 1,682,365 in 1921 to 5,621,715 in 1929.[45] Consumers had to be given a reason to replace perfectly fine cars with new models every few years.

Alfred P. Sloan came to General Motors as a director on November 7, 1918, rising to president by 1923.[46] With him came a new idea for marketing automobiles. Technology was a fine thing and needed to be improved. However, cars had to be "sold" to the public. Image soon would be the driving force in car sales.

> The trend from 1923-1927 meant a basic shift of the industry's attitude to the market. Henceforth the motorcars would have to be sold, instead of merely demonstrated. They must be advertised and serviced better. Research and improved methods of manufacturing would have to be constantly speeded up to produce better and better cars for a market ever growing more sternly competitive....Such increase in volume as developed would have to come from three sources: replacements, population growth, and the increased use of automobiles. Moreover, the share of business received by any producer would have to be secured through hard work and careful planning rather than through luck, boldness, or blind reliance on general prosperity.[47]

Planned obsolescence is a two pronged method of marketing products, particularly automobiles. The engineers were charged with mechanically improving their cars each year, so that a three year old car was inferior to the new model. Stylists sculpted sheet metal and crafted interiors that made the current model look vastly more modern than cars even a few years old. At the same time, the marketing department created a sense among the public that its company's products were an essential part of modern life. No self-respecting American wanted to be thought of as being less sophisticated and well-to-do than his neighbor, so the ploy generally worked. Many technological changes have occurred over the history of the automobile, but the basic design has remained remarkably similar. A 1941 Cadillac can carry five passengers from Indiana to California just as effectively as a current model can. The only differences lie in some technological "improvements" made to the design over the course of six decades.

Another key to General Motors success starting in the 1920s was the ladder concept. Alfred P. Sloan envisioned a young couple buying a Chevrolet as their first new car. As their fortunes rose, they ascended the GM ladder. The next rung was Pontiac, followed by

Oakland, Oldsmobile, Viking, Marquette, Buick, and LaSalle. When they finally reached the pinnacle of economic success, Cadillac was waiting for them. In the 1930 model year, General Motors produced ten distinct lines of cars, ranging in price from $495 for a base Chevrolet, to $9,700 for Cadillac V-16.[48] When Mr. Sloan sold a Chevrolet to a consumer, he fully expected someday that he would sell him a Cadillac.

General Motors cars always had a "family" look to them, but this became more evident after 1936 when the company began utilizing a limited number of bodies. Consider the 1941 line. All five cars have clear similarities in design. From Cadillac down to Chevrolet, the cars were clearly in the same styling line. The latter is much smaller, less powerful, and less well appointed than the former, but the similarities in styling are striking, particularly in the dash. This was no mistake. Cadillac by 1941 had acquired a reputation as being the most technologically advanced car in the luxury field. This prestige was used by General Motors to instill lesser priced lines with the image of quality enjoyed by Cadillac. This tactic would be used to an even greater extent after World War II.

Chapter 2 Notes

26   McCall, 67.

27   Cadillac Motor Car Division, *Cadillac Participation in the World War*, 11, 19-21.

28   Ibid., 21-22.

29   Ibid., 10.

30   Ibid., 14.

31   Ibid., 9.

32   Ibid., 14.

33   Ibid., 24.

34   McCall, 69.

35   Leland, 178.

36   Cadillac Motor Car Division, *Cadillac Participation in the World War*, 37, 39, 43. ##

37   Ibid., 47.

38   Ibid, 51.

39   McCall, 72.

40   Ibid.

41   Paul Ayres, "The Demise of the Cadillac Clark Avenue Plant:1921-1995, *The Classic Car,* March 1999, 46-48.

42   Pound, 224.

43   McCall, 129.

44   Pound, 268-269.

45   Ibid., 216.

46   Ibid., 205-208.

47   Ibid., 210.

48   Arthur J. Kuhn, *GM passes Ford, 1918-1938: designing the General Motors performance-control system* (University Park, PA: Pennsylvania State University Press, 1986), 86.

Chapter 3

Battle of the Supercars 1929-1940

The high times of the 1920s brought out the competitive spirit among luxury car manufacturers. Throughout the latter years of the decade, the groundwork was laid for what would be known as the "cylinder wars." The key to victory in this conflict lay in producing cars with the greatest number of cylinders, largest cubic inch displacement, and highest horsepower rating. At the time, they were status symbols of the ultra rich. Today, these cars are coveted by collectors as relics of the greatest era of motordom.

The Great Cylinder War

Philosopher Thorestein Veblen would have undoubtedly noted that the supercars were manifestations of conspicuous consumption. The cheapest body style in most manufacturers' catalog was the two passenger coupe. However, when the normally small coupe body was mounted on the same chassis as a limousine and powered by a massive engine, it lost its thriftiness. The towncar was the most glaring example of conspicuous consumption. Not only was it chauffer driven, but the driver sat in an exposed compartment for all the world to see.[49] During the boom times of the 1920s, such displays were almost essential for some in the upper class.

Buyers of these supercars demanded that their new vehicles' performance meet or exceed the ostentatiousness of their custom bodies. The Cadillac V-16, the Duesenberg, Marmon Sixteen and Packard Twelve all had top speeds in the one hundred miles per hour range. This was phenomenal considering that all of these cars weighed in excess of two tons. Even more surprising was the silence in which they moved at speed.[50] Modern luxury car owners would be pleased.

Duesenberg

Fred and August Duesenberg had been producing high performance automobiles since the 1910s. Their first race car appeared at the Indianapolis Motor Speedway in May 1914. Duesenberg racers made quite a reputation for themselves on the track over the next decade. Thinking that racing success might be converted into financial success, the pair introduced a new luxury car, the Duesenberg Model A, in November 1920. After six years, the time was right to improve the Model A. Only a dozen of the improved Model X Duesenbergs were built in 1927.[51] There rare cars paved the way for the ultimate supercar, the Model J Duesenberg.

The first shot in the cylinder war rang out from a humble plant at the corner of Washington and Harding in Indianapolis in May 1928. E.L. Cord, Harold Ames, and Al Leamy sent blueprints of their new supercar to nine of America's finest coach builders, including Derham, Murphy, and LeBaron. These custom bodies would rest upon chassis ranging from 149.5 inches to 160.5 inches, the longest in world. Power was provided by Fred and Augie Duesenberg's 420 cubic inch inline eight cylinder engine, the most advanced eight in the world. Producing 265 horsepower through standard carburetion and 400 though supercharging, the Duesenberg was not matched in sheer power for nearly thirty years.[52]

Mr. Cord, who had rescued Auburn Automobile Company from oblivion a few years earlier, believed that he could sell five hundred of these magnificent Model J Duesenbergs annually, even with an $8,500 base price for the chassis alone.[53] The prolonged good times of the 1920s might have made him believe this for a while, but the stock market collapse of 1929 shattered those dreams. Slightly more than five hundred Duesenbergs were made during the entire eight year production run, the last waiting until April 1940 to have a body mounted.[54] These cars went to the rich and famous. Clark Gable and Gary Cooper drove Model Js. Industrialists from such diverse backgrounds as Ethel Mars and Cliff Durant made room for them in their garages.[55] The upper crust in other nations also enjoyed the prestige of the Duesenberg, including Indian potentate Maharajah Holkar.[56] In the end, the ultra high society market simply wasn't strong enough to support cars that often cost more than a fine new house.

Marmon

Marmon Motor Car Company was headquartered north of Monument Circle in Indianapolis. The marque's claim to fame was producing the car that won the first Indianapolis 500 in 1911. The firm began work on a V-16 as early as 1925, but progress had been slow. 1929 brought the introduction of the lower priced Roosevelt, an attempt to make the marque more accessible to the public. The company turned a $1,000,000 profit that year.[57] In late 1930, the new Marmon Sixteen debuted at the Paris Automobile Salon. Fitted with a LeBaron body designed by then-nineteen year old M.I.T. student Walter Dorwin Teague Jr., the car sat for most of the show obscured by a Judkins bodied Lincoln. The real test would come in New York City.[58]

MoToR magazine raved about the Marmon Sixteen's all aluminum, 200 horsepower, 490.8 cubic inch engine. So advanced was the power plant that company founder Howard Marmon was awarded the Moskovics Medal for outstanding achievement in the field of engineering.[59] While the press adulation was wonderful for Mr. Marmon's ego, it didn't erase the fact that Cadillac had beaten him to the punch with the V-16. The first Marmon Sixteen arrived in showrooms in February 1931. Production was slow and costly. Three hundred skilled workers labored two full days to produce one car.[60] By 1933, the Marmon motorcar would be no more. A subsidiary, Marmon-Herrington Company, continued on for a few more decades, producing all wheel drive truck chassis.[61]

Packard

Packard had built a V-12 as late as 1923, but had abandoned it as being impractical.[62] A new twelve cylinder engine was introduced in 1932. It was a rather late entry into the cylinder war. 1932 would be one of the worst years that the auto industry had yet seen. Packard had no choice but to produce a supercar of some sort just to stay even with its rivals in terms of prestige. The Packard Twelve was destined to have a short production life, seeing the last one trundle down the assembly line in 1939. All told, slightly more than 6,000 were produced during this time, a far cry from the 10,000 V-12s built by Cadillac from 1931 to 1937.[63]

Packard survived the Depression by venturing into the middle price range in 1932. Three years later, the company moved into that bracket with a vengeance, producing a smaller car powered by a smaller inline eight cylinder engine than its more expensive cousins. In 1937, a companion six cylinder powered model was introduced. These cars were aimed at Buick and Oldsmobile owners rather than Cadillac buyers. They were as well engineered as their more expensive brothers, but were smaller and less well appointed. This is not to say that the Junior Packards were small vehicles. They still had enough headroom for a six-foot-tall driver to wear his hat while at the wheel.[64] Packard was right in the short term to build the economical Model 110 and 115 sixes, as well as the 120 and Clipper Eights, in huge numbers. The larger 160 and 180 series cars simply could not be sold in great enough quantities to keep the company solvent in the face of perilous economic times. Although it is often noted that Packard handily outsold Cadillac during the pre-war period, closer scrutiny of the sales data disproves this myth. The "Junior" Packards amounted to ninety four percent of company sales during some years. If one considers only equivalent models, Cadillac outsold Packard in 1930, 1931, 1936, 1937, 1938, 1939, 1940, 1941, and 1942. While promoting the Junior series cars helped the company survive the Depression, Packard paid the price in prestige. After World War II, Packard was known primarily as a high quality middle priced car.[65]

Multicylinder Cadillacs

Cadillac Motor Car Company President Lawrence P. Fisher stunned his dealers two months after the stock market crash with the announcement of the widely anticipated V-16. The new car, an Imperial Landau sedan, debuted at the 1930 New York Auto Show on January 4. Cadillac engine guru Owen Nacker designed the mighty 452 cubic inch power plant. It was rated at 165 horsepower, and was capable of pushing these massive cars to 100 miles per hour. The engine was essentially a pair of eight cylinder engines tied together with a common crankshaft, each bank having its own fuel and exhaust systems. The overhead valve engine was nearly silent at idle. Polished aluminum, chrome, and porcelain covers kept all unsightly engine parts hidden from view. The Cadillac V-16 was available in fifty four semi-custom Fleetwood built body styles. Of the 4,403 cars built between 1930 and 1940, 2,887 were sold during the 1930 model year.[66] The remaining 1,019 first generation V-16s were built through 1937.

In October 1937, a new generation of V-16 was introduced at the New York Auto Show. Unlike its predecessor, this engine was an L-head. The valves were located inside the block, operated by a bank of lifters acting directly from the camshaft. Gone was the complicated overhead valve train, with its series of pushrods, rocker arms and shafts. This resulted in a much simpler engine design. The engine was of monobloc construction, meaning that all sixteen cylinders and the crankcase were cast as one unit. This was considerably lighter than the earlier design, where the cylinders bolted to the crankcase. The weight savings were considerable, shaving 250 pounds off the powertrain. The new V-16 was six inches shorter than the previous incarnation. It was also considerably more humble looking, painted the same olive drab as the lesser priced V-8. There were no polished aluminum sparkplug wire covers. Instead, a very utilitarian 135 degree V-16 crouched in the engine bay. It was so flat that part of it was slid underneath the firewall, allowing for a shorter car while retaining the interior space as its predecessor.[67] The only disadvantage with the new V-16 was the primitive nature of casting technology available in 1937. Tiny cracks appeared in the blocks after they cooled. Sand sometimes got into places where it was not intended to be. Today, technology exists to correct the problem during restoration, but the original owners were not as fortunate.

What is most remarkable is that Cadillac President Nick Dreystadt knew that the company would be lucky to sell fifty examples annually. When the sales tallies were in, he must have been delighted to find that the new car did better than expected. Cadillac sold 311 V-16s in sixteen body styles in 1938, followed by 135 units the next year. The final year, 1940, saw fifty one cars sold, with an additional ten engines produced and not fitted to chassis.[68] He had his reasons for continuing the program long after it was clear that it was a losing proposition. Automotive historian Walter M.P. McCall offers some insight into the reasoning at Cadillac.

> While it is doubtful that General Motors made money from the V-16 program, this magnificent series undoubtedly did much for GM. It clearly established Cadillac as the new American luxury car leader and bestowed upon Cadillac an image, an aura of mystique that continues to surround the marque to this day. The Cadillac V-16 was a monumental piece of automotive engineering, the likes of which have not been seen since.[69]

Mr. McCall may have overstated his case for the V-16 leading to market dominance, as Packard still had a few good sales years ahead of it during the 1940s. His point is well taken in that the image of Cadillac as luxury leader was forged during the Great Depression, with the actual move to complete dominance waiting until the coming of peace.

In the end, the cylinder wars did more harm than good for most manufacturers. Duesenberg, Marmon, Pierce Arrow, and Peerless all perished during the Great Depression. As impressive as these cars were, they simply were not practical to produce during a time of economic turmoil. By investing in models that there was no hope of getting a return on their investment, these companies insured that they would not live to see 1940.[70]

Chapter 3 Notes

49 Jim Crabtree, "Conspicuous Consumption and Classic Cars," *The Classic Car,* December 1998, 18-19.

50 Maurice D. Hendry, "Comparing the Performance of Classic 'Muscle' Cars," *The Classic Car,* September 1999, 51.

51 Mike Mueller, "1927 Duesenberg Straight 8- The little-known Model X," *Cars and Parts,* July 2002, 29-31.

52 Beverly Rae Kimes, *The Classic Era* (Des Plaines, Illinois: Classic Car Club of America, 2001), 114.

53 Ibid.

54 Eric Brockman, "One Man's Art: Rudolf Bauer and the last Duesenberg," *Cars and Parts,* July 1995, 26.

55 Nina Padgett, "1932 Duesenberg Torpedo: back home in Indiana," *Car Collector and Car Classics,* June 1993, 32.

Phil Skinner, "The Town Car: Under the skin, it's still a Duesenberg," *Cars and Parts,* July 1997, 54.

56 Nicky Wright, "The Adventures of CUW109: The tale of a much- traveled Duesenberg," *Car Collector and Car Classics,* November 1980,36.

57 Kimes, 158.

58 Ibid., 188.

59 Ibid., 190.

60 Eric Kaminsky, "1931 Marmon V-16 Coupe," *Cars and Parts,* February 2003, 17.

61 George E. Orwig II, "Marmon: The Final Chapter," *Antique Automobile,* July- August 1997, 13.

62 "1923 Packard, " Packard Club website; available from http://www.packardclub.org; Internet; accessed 30 May, 2005.

63 "Packard Twelve," Packard Club website; available from http://wwwpackardcluborg; Internet; accessed 30 May, 2005.

64 Jim Richardson, "A Packard for the Proletariat," *Classic Auto Restorer,* June 1992,62.

65 "Junior Series Packard, "Packard Club website; available from http://www.packardclub.org; Internet; accessed 30 May, 2005.

[66] McCall, 143-144

[67] Ibid., 222-223.

[68] Terry Wenger, "Survivor! the Story of the 1938-1940 Cadillac V-16," *The Classic Car,* Autumn 2004, 7.

[69] McCall, 223.

[70] Darrell Davis, "The First Eight-Cylinder Chrysler Imperials," *The Classic Car,* Summer 2005, 26.

Chapter 4

Personal Luxury is Born
1935-1940

In the mid 1930s, a new idea arose in Auburn, Indiana. From the very early years of the century, it had been considered important for luxury cars to be chauffer driven for the sake of prestige. However, E.L. Cord had a different idea. He believed that some of the elite might like to drive their own cars, as long as they had the same amenities as larger automobiles. The idea of a personal luxury car was born in January 1934. After a year and a half of development, the first Cord prototypes were ready for testing in July 1935, with production models arriving in showrooms in 1936.[71] The Cord was expensive at $2,000, but was designed to be driven by the owner. It sat much lower than any car on the road, had front wheel drive, concealed headlights, and no running boards. For the owner's enjoyment, Cords had electric shifting as a standard feature, with an optional supercharger for added pep. Had the Auburn Automobile Company not already been in its death throes, many more than 2,000 examples would certainly have been produced.

At twenty-four, Bill Mitchell was a relatively young man in the stylist field. Despite this, he was charged by General Motors' chief designer Harley Earl with creating a car along the lines of the Cord.[72] Although initially designed as a LaSalle, the car was produced as a Cadillac The result was the 1938 Series 60 Special. Built on the smallest and least expensive chassis offered by Cadillac, it sat lower than any other car then in production. The grill was wide, giving the front an impressive stance. The doors were a two piece affair, mimicking the appearance of a convertible. Chrome trim was kept to a minimum, with no belt moldings to break the continuity of the design. As in the Cord, no running boards were fitted.[73] It was clearly marketed to the owner/driver, as seen in period advertisements. In the 1939 ad "500 Miles- and still an hour to sunset," the sunglasses-wearing owner commented to his wife about the speed and efficiency of his new Cadillac while the couple were motoring through the desert. The copy noted that owners said that the 60 Special rode and handled better than other cars, inspiring confidence in both the driver and passenger.[74]

The first generation Series 60 Specials were produced from 1938 to 1941, with a high percentage surviving to the present day. Ironically, the formerly light and nimble Series 60 Specials eventually evolved into the Fleetwood Brougham. At the time of the model's demise in 1996, it was the top of the line, least nimble car in Cadillac's catalog.[75]

The Continental is born- 1939

Edsel Ford loved sports cars and wanted to incorporate them into the Ford production line. Early 1930s chassis were too tall and too long to do as he wished. Luckily, the new 1938 Lincoln Zephyr provided just the foundation that he needed. It had a shallow floor pan that would help give the car the lower profile that Mr. Ford desired. He put E.T. "Bob" Gregorie to work on styling the car. Gregorie gave it a raked windshield, long fenders, and a low roofline, producing a car that looked sportier, at least on paper. With a March 1939 deadline to get the project finished looming ahead, the prototype was hand built from sketches and a clay model. The only problem with the design is that there was no space for a spare tire in the trunk. This was solved by mounting it outside above the rear bumper. Edsel Ford like the car so much that he commissioned four more prototypes to study the practicality of putting the design into production.[76] The Lincoln Continental was born.

The long hood/short rear deck Lincoln was ready for production by 1940. Due to expense and time needed to create each convertible, only twenty-five had been built by the end of 1939. The pace picked up considerable after the new year, but only 350 convertibles and fifty-four coupes had been completed by the end of the 1940 model year. Each unit sold for $2,840, over a thousand dollars more than a regular Lincoln Zephyr convertible. Despite this, the company lost money on every car sold. Radically modern good looks aside, the underpinnings of this new personal luxury car were very traditional. The Continental used the same obsolescent transverse springs and solid front axle that other Fords would retain until 1949.[77]

The 1941 model year, beginning on September 20, 1940, would be much more prosperous for Lincoln.[78] Continental sales grew to 1,250, of which 800 were coupes and the remainder were convertibles.[79] Although sales were good, difficulties with the small V-12 power plant began to manifest themselves. Water flow was very poor, causing overheating problems. This led to cylinder bore warpage and excessive ring wear. Crankcase ventilation was also under par, resulting in higher sludge buildup in the oil pan. Oil flow was restricted, shortening engine life. Hydraulic lifters and cast iron heads helped solve some of these problems by 1942, but the damage to Lincoln's reliability reputation had already been done.[80] The Continental returned after World War II for three additional seasons with some improvements, but production remained low.

Personal Luxury at Packard

Packard took a similar approach to personal luxury as Lincoln. Open cars, not sedans, were the basis for Packard's personal luxury cars. Customers who wanted something a little different shipped their new Packards to custom body builders who would translate dreams to sheet metal. Derham or Rollson worked with East Coast clients, while Bohman & Schwartz labored in Pasadena, California. These custom bodies cost upwards of $6,000, limiting their ownership to the richest families in the nation. The stratospheric price-tag also kept orders under 100 per year.[81]

Packard did sanction a small number of factory customs. "Dutch" Darrin built his first Packard based custom in 1937 for actor Dick Powell. Soon, Clark Gable, Rosalind Russell, and Al Jolson lined up to get their Darrin customized Packards.[82] Management at the company undoubtedly saw an opportunity to produce an ultra-luxury/personal luxury car that would attract buyers to the showroom. If these cars were officially sponsored by the factory, Packard might have been able to use Hollywood glamour to help sell more of the lower priced Packards. This hope was at least partially borne out by the fact that showroom floor traffic increased by 300% in dealerships that had one of Darrin's cars on display.[83] Although a sedan could be ordered, the vast majority of customers preferred open cars. These were handsome convertibles, with raked windshields and the fabled "Darrin Dip" in the doors. The Darrins were strictly for the extremely wealthy who enjoyed driving. Production numbers reflect this. Only forty-seven Darrins of all types were built for 1940, another thirty-five in 1941, and a final fifteen for 1942.[84] Despite this scarcity, the concept of the Packard Darrin proved that the public wanted personal luxury, albeit with an extremely large price tag.

It is interesting to note that Packard did not make quite as serious an attempt to capture this market as Cadillac had done. The famous Packard Darrins of 1940-1942 were owner driven, but those owners were often Hollywood's elite. The Junior models were aimed squarely at the middle price field. Even the Clipper, the closest Packard came to the Series 60 Special, lacked the amenities of the Cadillac, and was more in line with the older Junior models.[85] This misstep by Packard would cost them dearly after World War II.

War clouds were looming on the horizon as the 1930s drew to a close. The annexation of Austria and the Sudatenland were cause for concern. Most auto manufacturers were hoping for a return to the good times like those before the Crash in 1929. Cadillac was well on its way to becoming the premiere luxury car at the dawn of the 1940s. The company's long history of precision and innovation certainly helped in this matter. Cadillac's service during World War I in the air and on the ground reinforced its reputation for ruggedness. The meaning of luxury had been redefined by Cadillac during the 1930s with the introduction of the ultra-expensive V-16 at the beginning of the decade. Eight years later, after vanquishing several competitors, the company again changed the meaning of luxury by wresting the steering wheel away from chauffeur and placing it in the owner's hands. Many in the industry hoped that 1941 would be the first in a series of successful years that would usher in another golden age. Cadillac was ready to take charge of the entire upper price class, barring any unforeseen events.

Chapter 4 Notes

71 Josh B. Malks, *Cord 810/812: The Timeless Classic* (Iola, Wisconsin: Krause Publications, 1995), 24, 74-75

72 Richard Stanley, "What's so special about the 1938 Sixty Special? Part I," *The Self Starter,* April 2003, 12-13.

74 Joel Prescott, "After the Ball," *The Classic Car,* December 2000, 12.

75 Richard Stanley, "What's so special about the 1938 Sixty Special? Part III," *The Self Starter,* June 2003 , 11.

76 West Peterson, "1939 Lincoln Continental: One more notch for Edsel and Gregorie," *Cars and Parts,* March 2003, 12-14.

77 Arch Brown, "Black Beauty: 1941 Lincoln Continental Coupe," *Cars and Parts,* January 1998, 52-53.

78 Kimes, 639.

79 Brown, "Black Beauty: 1941 Lincoln Continental Coupe, 54.

80 West Peterson, "1946 Lincoln Continental Cabriolet: Being seen in a personal luxury automobile," *Cars and Parts,* March 2000, 35.

81 Bob Stevens, "Bohman & Schwartz customizes a '40 Packard," *Cars and Parts,* February 1998, 47-48.

82 Richard M. Langworth, "The Packard Darrins: Immortal creations of a breakaway designer," *Collectable Automobile,* June 1992, 30.

83 Ibid., 34.

84 Ibid.

85 Kimes, 626.

Part II

Cadillac Goes To War:
The Homefront

The early 1940s would be a pivotal time in Cadillac's ongoing campaign to dominate the fine car field. The fresh 1941 models set the tone for the decade with their new technology and high styling. As sales receipts for that year show, the public embraced the new definition of modern luxury. Had World War II not occurred, it is quite probable that Cadillac would have come to dominate the field within a few years. The war brought a number of benefits to the company. While its primary rival, Packard, was busy making aircraft and marine engines, Cadillac continued to field test its improved engine and transmission and had new tooling was installed at Clark Avenue with the War Department footing the bill. When the war ended, Cadillac had an improved product and a modern factory, while Packard had to spend millions of dollars retooling. Additionally, Cadillac's work building components for Allison aircraft engines allowed stylists to legitimately tap into the public's infatuation with aviation during the first few decades after the war. World War II allowed Cadillac to build on the advances of 1941, both technologically and stylistically, without the company producing a single car for three years.

Chapter 5

The '41s arrive
October 1940

A freshly restyled line arrived in Cadillac showrooms in October 1940. The day of finally seizing total control of the luxury field from Packard seemed to be at hand. Excitement in the buying public about the new 1941 Cadillac was hard to ignore. The company not seen anything like this since the halcyon days of the Roaring Twenties.

> From day one, spontaneous and unprecedented rave reviews poured in from every quarter. Telegrams of congratulations literally stacked up at the Clark plant. Factory branch retail stores in New York, Chicago and Detroit were overwhelmed by enthusiasm for the new models. In Los Angeles and San Francisco, the showrooms of Cadillac distributor Don Lee were packed with visitors- on the first day over 100 retail orders were logged in a matter of hours. A similar scenario played out at dealerships throughout the nation.[86]

October 1940 was the best sales month on record at Cadillac Motors, outstripping the previous record by six hundred units. By November, 23,000 orders had been placed, and Cadillac President Dreystadt announced a twenty percent increase in production just to meet demand.[87] As far as the company was concerned, the lean times of the 1930s had finally come to an end.

To some casual observers, however, 1941 might appear to have been a year of retrenchment. The LaSalle, the faithful stablemate to Cadillac since 1927, was gone. After eleven seasons, the prestigious V-16 had passed from the scene as well. In their place were six series all powered by the same engine.[88] Cadillac-LaSalle had offered no less than four separate powerplants as late as 1937. The LaSalle had served its purpose well, preventing car buyers from defecting from GM during the transition from upper middle priced cars to the luxury bracket. The V-16 had also succeeded, undoubtedly handing victory to Cadillac during the cylinder wars of the 1930s. Apparent retrenchment was, in fact, consolidation.

Just as General Motors had a ladder leading customers from Chevrolet up to Cadillac, each company had a similar system of its own. Cadillac's hierarchy ranged from the low priced 61 Series coupe up to the expensive and exclusive 75 Series limousine. Once buyers arrived at Cadillac, Mr. Dreystadt was determined that they would stay there, providing models for a variety of tastes and prices. In the case of the lower priced series like the 61 and 62, each model had standard and deluxe versions. For 1941, the LaSalle's place was taken by the 61 Series.[89] Four models of the fastback body were offered, starting at $1,275 for the base 6127 five passenger coupe rising to $1,460 for the 6109D deluxe five passenger sedan. 29,250 examples were sold during the model year, making the Series 61 the most popular Cadillac model.[90]

Owners who still wanted to drive their cars, but also desired greater interior space, chose the Series 62. The "C" bodyshell was in its second season in 1941. This "torpedo" body was widely popular in 1940 and was retained with changes made to the auxiliary sheetmetal. Customers had a choice of standard or deluxe coupes and sedans, a convertible coupe, a convertible sedan, and a commercial chassis.[91] Prices for the 62 Series ranged from $1345 for a 6227 five passenger standard coupe to $1,875 for the convertible sedan. Cadillac produced 24,726 examples of the series for 1941.[92]

A new LaSalle Special was planned for 1941. A September 1940 *Cadillac Salesman's Databook* illustration of the new heating system clearly shows an overhead shot of a car that has the LaSalle's characteristic narrow grille.[93] The decision not produce the new model was probably made at the very last moment. The new body, a fastback like the Series 61, became the Series 63.[94] Only one model, a five passenger sedan was offered.[95] It appeared solely in deluxe form, retailing for $1,605. Cadillac sold 5,050 owner driven 63 Series sedans in 1941.[96]

The first incarnation of Bill Mitchell's fabled 1938 tour de force, the Series 60 Special, lasted four seasons. The original intent of producing a personal luxury car was truly fulfilled in this model. Of all the cars produced by Cadillac in 1941, the 60 Specials stand out as the most unique of the line. Few, if any, of the 4,100 cars produced that year are identical.[97] Power divider windows and air conditioning were installed on a number of 60 Specials.[98] These options quickly drove the price above the base of $2,085.[99] These were some of the last examples of custom automobiles produced by General Motors. The 60 Special was the ultimate owner driven luxury car, complete with many of the amenities that modern drivers enjoy.

With the demise of the V-16, one might expect that the options for the ultra-wealthy would have been significantly reduced at Cadillac. Such was not the case. A new formal sedan, the Series 67, replaced the aging Series 75 body of 1937-1940. It was a fastback, sharing its body with Buick's Series 90 sedan.[100] Only 900 examples left the showroom floor, priced from $2,470 to $2,760.[101] Unlike the previously mentioned models, the Series 67 was intended to be chauffer driven, making it the very model of an old-line luxury car, with a hint of modernity.

The crown jewel of the Cadillac line for 1941 was the new Series 75. In reality, the "new" body was the previous model year's Series 72 with modernized fenders, hood, and deck lid. With room for up to nine passengers, the Series 75 was priced from $2,895 to $4,045, depending upon the options selected by the customer. Over 2,100 found their way to the carriage houses of America's finest families in 1941.[102] It is quite likely that few of these owners ever found themselves behind the wheel of their Series 75 sedan. This model was a traditionalist's luxury car.

It was clear very early that the 1941 model year was destined to be one of Cadillac's finest. The 1941 Cadillac's contribution to the marque's post war dominance was almost as significant as that of the V-16. The modern, personal luxury concept of 1938 had really taken hold by 1941. Only 3,004 traditional, chauffer driven Cadillacs were produced that year. The remainder of production, 63,126 units, was comprised of owner driven cars. Cadillac had made the transition to the modern ideal of luxury, proven by the simple fact that traditional luxury cars were outsold by personal luxury models by a factor of twenty to one. Today, 1941 is one of the most popular Cadillac model years with collectors. They are prized not only for their stunning good looks on the show field, but also have proven their worth on the touring circuit. The design is nearly perfectly balanced, with the sculpted sheet metal accented by the right amount of chrome trim. Seventeen exterior colors were offered.[103] Two tone paint jobs were becoming more common, making many 1941 Cadillacs an esthetic joy.

One of the reasons for the success is the modernity of the car. 1941 was the first year that the Hydra-Matic automatic transmission was installed in Cadillacs, an option selected by nearly one third of buyers. By twenty-first century standards, the shifting is rather harsh. At the time, it was considered to be novel and quite reliable. Steering on the '41 Cadillac is as light and responsive as any non-power assisted steering can be. Seats are comfortable with adequate leg room for front and rear passengers, even in the coupes. Heaters were still not universal in 1941, but most Cadillacs had them. Some Series 60 Specials had metal sliding sunroofs, dubbed "Sunshine Turret Tops," installed.[104] The '41 Cadillac was a thrifty car, delivering up to fourteen miles per gallon, a very respectable figure well into the 1970s.[105] A handful of cars, the bulk of which were Series 75 sedans, were fitted with air conditioning, a very modern option. Unlike later automotive air conditioners, these early Frigidaire units had no clutch on the compressor. As a result, there was no control over cooling. The faster the car went, the cooler the cabin grew. In winter, the system had to be partially dismantled to prevent unpleasant coldness for the passengers.[106] Prior to the introduction of the personal luxury concept, these things were of little concern to owners of fine cars. Ease of handling and maintenance were details best left to chauffeurs. With the owner acting as the driver, he was much more aware of these issues. Personal luxury would be the hallmark of the post war fine car field, and Cadillac was far ahead of its competitors.

Even with the good times of 1941, all was not well at Cadillac. At the beginning of production, France, Norway, and the Low Countries had already fallen to the might of the Wehrmacht. While hundreds of new Cadillacs rolled off the line at Clark Avenue, London was being pounded nightly by the Luftwaffe. Nick Dreystadt and his associates wished that the good times could go on forever, but that didn't look likely. Even the company's showroom catalog for 1941 cast doubt on the future. "For thirty-nine years, Cadillac's manufacturing policy has remained one of the few certain things in an uncertain world."[107] The 1941 model year would go into the record books as the most profitable year yet at Cadillac. 1942 would have a uniqueness of its own.

Chapter 5 Notes

[86] Schneider, *Cadillacs of the Forties*, 39.

[87] Ibid., 39.

[88] Cadillac Motor Car Division, *Operating Hints for the 1941 Cadillac* (Detroit, Michigan: General Motors Sales Corporation, 1940), 24.

[89] Cadillac Motor Car Division, *Cadillac and Cadillac Fleetwood for 1941* (Detroit, Michigan: Service Department, Cadillac Motor Car Division, 1940), 4.

[90] Schneider, *Cadillacs of the Forties*, 178.

[91] Cadillac Motor Car Division, *Cadillac and Cadillac Fleetwood for 1941*, 3.

[92] Schneider, *Cadillacs of the Forties*, 178.

[93] Cadillac Motor Car Division, *1941 Cadillac Salesman's Databook* (Detroit Michigan: General Motors Sales Corporation, September 17, 1940), 98.

[94] Ron Van Gelderen and Matt Larson, *LaSalle: Cadillac's Companion Car* (Paducah, Kentucky: Turner Publishing, 2000), 352-362.

[95] Cadillac Motor Car Division, *Cadillac and Cadillac Fleetwood for 1941*, 7.

[96] Schneider, *Cadillacs of the Forties*, 178.

[97] Ibid.

[98] Nineteen Forty-One Authenticity Team. *Authenticity Manual, Class 11- 1941 Cadillac* (Columbus, Ohio: Cadillac-LaSalle Club, Inc., 2004), A-11.

[99] Schneider, *Cadillacs of the Forties*, 178.

[100] Cadillac Motor Car Division, *Cadillac and Cadillac Fleetwood for 1941*, 8.

[101] Schneider, *Cadillacs of the Forties*, 178.

[102] Ibid.

[103] Sherwin Williams Automotive Finishes, "1941 Cadillac Passenger Car Production Colors," paint code sheet, Sherwin Williams Corporation, 1941.

[104] McCall, 248.

[105] Cadillac Motor Car Division, *Cadillac and Cadillac Fleetwood for 1941*, 13.

[106] Cadillac Motor Car Division, *Cadillac Air Conditioning Manual* (Detroit, Michigan: Service Department, Cadillac Motor Car Division, 1941), 5-13.

[107] Cadillac Motor Car Division, *Cadillac and Cadillac Fleetwood for 1941*, 1.

Chapter 6

War Comes to the Dealers 1942-1945

Cadillac hoped to top its 1941 success the next year. The 1942 line-up, encompassing twenty two body styles within six series, was more streamlined than its predecessors. The fenders on all series, except the Series 75, extended into the front doors, creating the first modern "pontoon" fenders mounted on a Cadillac.[108] This look would remain in vogue until 1950.

Cadillac sales literature now mentioned the company's defense work. Very early in the 1942 showroom catalog, talk turned from the usual sales pitch for a new car to something more somber. A trio of Army Air Force fighters, a P-38, a P-39, and a P-40, winged their way across the page.

> Two years ago, Cadillac was awarded an even more signal honor. Cadillac was selected for one of the most exacting and important manufacturing operations in all of industry- the production of precision parts for the power plant of some of America's greatest military planes, the famed Allison engine. Immediately accepted as Cadillac's

major responsibility, production of these vital parts was soon underway, and has exceeded schedule almost from the start. Already a considerable part of the Cadillac plant is devoted entirely to Allison engine production, and more men and facilities will be added as fast as the nation's need requires. Meanwhile-and for as along as it can be done without interfering withNational Defense- Cadillac will fulfill its obligation to the thousands who look to Cadillac for the ultimate in personal transportation.[109]

There was no mention of Cadillac's contract to build tanks for the U.S. Army. The Allison engine project had been underway since 1939, so it was no longer a secret. The new tank design was still under development when the catalog was sent to dealers in September 1941.

The unprovoked sneak attack on Pearl Harbor abruptly ended Cadillac's hopes for a stellar 1942 model year. Most civilian automobile production had ended by February 5, 1942. Only 16,511 Cadillacs were produced during the abbreviated 1942 model year, a respectable total for four months' production.[110] The company shifted its goal from defeating Packard and Lincoln in the marketplace to vanquishing fascism and militarism on the battlefield.

Shortages

While Cadillac publicly hoped for a better 1942 model year, the die was cast long before the first bombs fell on Oahu. Material shortages occurred as early as October 1940, with some aluminum alloys becoming hard to find.[111] The situation worsened by the following May. More than half a billion pounds of critical metals were shifted from civilian to military production.

In the passenger car total is 118,000,000 pounds of zinc; more than 20,000,000 pounds of aluminum; a total of nickel in excess of 11,000,00 pounds, including that which would be used in the

186,000,000 pounds of nickel steel which would be released.[112]

There was even talk in the auto industry of scouring salvage yards for junked cars that could then be smelted whole as a source for increasingly scarce steel.[113]

Cadillac felt the pinch throughout the 1941 model year. With a fair amount of chrome trim on the division's cars, it was hard for Nick Dreystadt and company to imagine a world without zinc. This metal was critical for the war effort. Zinc based pigments were used in camouflage paints and for corrosion protection on aircraft.[114] The lower zinc content in the potmetal grilles, fender spears, and other trim did not cause problems initially. Over time, however, the chrome plating broke down on these items, causing pitting. One of the biggest expenses that modern restorers face with these cars is at the chrome shop, thanks in great part from the material shortages of 1941-42.

There was no real hope that the automobile industry would sell more cars in 1942 than in the previous year. The War Production Board announced in February 1941 that no more non-defense tooling could legally be purchased by manufacturers. Auto production was to be limited to one half 1941 levels, or 3,460,000 units, dashing chances for a record-breaking 1942 sales year.[115]

In its December 7, 1941 issue, *Business Week* predicted a shutdown of civilian production the following February at the earliest and July at the latest. Manufacturers were having trouble getting steel for such crucial items as timing gears and bearings, thanks to government regulations.[116] In early November, 1941, the Office of Production Management issued Order L-2-b, declaring that auto manufacturers would not be able to produce cars with chrome trim after December 15. Copper was as big of a concern as zinc, since most cars had over fifty pounds of the metal per car.[117] This order was later relaxed by Conservation Order M-9-c, pushing the cut off date back to December 31 and exempting bumpers, wiper arms, door locks and lock covers, vent window latches, and body trim screws.[118] L.C. Cargile, President of National Automobile Dealers Association, predicted that this material shortage would work its way down to the dealer level and cause one quarter of the nation's 40,000 dealers to close by the end of 1942. The rest would have to rely on service to survive.[119] This gloomy outlook preceded the declaration of war by several days.

The final 2,150 civilian Cadillacs rolled out of Clark Avenue between January 21 and February 5, 1942. Chromium was at a premium, so the exterior trim was painted gunmetal gray. Over the next few days, an additional 719 ambulance chassis were produced to supply the nation's needs for the duration. Two months later, the first M-5 tank rolled off of the Cadillac assembly line, beginning a new chapter in the company's history.[120] The existence of this new tank had been revealed to the public a scant four months earlier.[121]

Saving the Dealers

While it was important to build up potential markets for the post war period, Cadillac had to insure that its network of dealers would survive the war. A handful of cars had been held back for release to essential personnel in 1943. These certainly wouldn't carry the company through the war. *Business Week* noted that dealer closures spiked in May and June 1942, due mostly to a shortage of cars to sell.[122] Cadillac launched a three prong attack against the problem. First, it would provide service for existing cars to allow them to stay on the road for the duration. Second, dealers would sell accessories that were not rationed. Finally, Cadillac's ad campaign during the war would emphasize the importance of the current work, while drawing ties both to the company's storied past and to the bright hopes for the future.

In late 1941, L.C. Cargile, pointed to the ways that the auto industry could survive an upcoming conflict.

> Keep them rolling- If automobile manufacturers have their way dealers will get parts- all they need- not only because parts are the lifeblood of the retail trade today but also because, when the emergency has passed, a manufacturer's best argument in rebuilding a dealer organization will be, "we kept our cars rolling through it all, didn't we?"[123]

Even in 1941, the number of tires being recapped had exploded over the previous year. Over 7,500,000 tires had been salvaged by retreading that year. *Business Week* noted that if the number of retreads could be moved to 12,000,000 for 1942, over 20,000 long tons of increasingly scarce rubber would be saved.[124]

The *Cadillac Serviceman* was an invaluable tool for dealers. Published bi-monthly, it helped the company keep its dealers and mechanics up to date with the latest changes from the factory. Shop manuals of the early 1940s were frustratingly general, and the *Serviceman* helped fill the gaps. During World War II, the publication advised its readers on the best ways to retain the loyalty of customers when no new cars were in sight.

In 1942, the *Serviceman* explained the problems with lower octane fuels, showed how to properly store new cars, and extolled the virtues of thorough inspections. Parts were to be sold only on an as needed basis to prevent hoarding. It warned dealers to follow the OPA regulations regarding service charges. "Break a Tool, Jap's Delight," a cartoon in the September-October issue drove home the importance of maintaining tools.[125]

For 1943, the emphasis was placed upon the importance of scrap metal. In the January-February issue, "Scrap is Ammunition" reminded dealers of this in cartoon form. In July, dealers learned that it took only ninety pounds of steel to keep a doughboy supplied in 1918, while his modern counterpart required 4,900 pounds. In September, it was revealed that the War Production Board's estimates for amount of scrap metal required to win the war had doubled over the past year.[126]

By 1944, two full years had passed since the last new Cadillac had rolled off the line. Each issue of the *Serviceman* featured a different system that might fail during wartime. In January, the Hydra-Matic transmission was highlighted. The vacuum actuated radio aerial was spotlighted in May. Throughout the year, the publication pushed the idea that superior service during the war would be the key to post war success.[127]

The other major concern of dealers, after service, was sales. Late model used cars quickly sold. With little else to sell, they turned to the accessory market. A significant number of radios, heaters, fog lights, back up lights and windshield washers had been produced prior to the end of civilian production. Automotive accessories were of no use to the military, but dealers found that they could make a little money by selling these items to their customers when they came in for regular maintenance.[128] Radios and heaters made the miles pass faster, even though the cars were limited to thirty five miles per hour on the highway. Fog lights made driving under blackout conditions a little safer. Back up lights, an option starting in 1941, warned those behind a Cadillac of its driver's intentions, helping to prevent costly accidents. Cadillac owners who had relatively new tires on their cars had good reason to fear thieves. For only $12.50, their local dealer would install wheel locks to deter ne'er do wells from plying their craft.[129] Cadillac promoted the sale of all these accessories with contests dubbed "Cadillac Victory Sweepstakes," promising prizes to superior performing salesmen.[130] This activity helped keep the dealers in business, waiting for the day when the new cars would start arriving.

General Motors had a variety of methods for keeping the public interested during the war years. In the spring of 1942, Cadillac sent out 150,000 "Mileage Manuals" to its customers, telling them how to get the most out of their cars.[131] The Customer Research Staff at General Motors published the first edition of *The Automobile User's Guide with Wartime Suggestions* in February 1942. Over the next two years, over 7,000,000 copies were distributed to the public.[132] Within its sixty five pages, drivers were instructed on the best ways to conserve precious gasoline, oil, tires, and mechanical parts. Proper driving habits were also reinforced. Only on the last page did an advertisement for GM's hoped for postwar plans appear. In an effort to keep its customer apprised of its wartime activities, the company published "Cadillac...from Peace to War" in 1944.[133] The pamphlet included enough hard data about the Allison V-1710 and the M-5 tank to make the reader feel informed, without disclosing any vital details that would jeopardize wartime secrecy. These direct mail campaigns helped lay the groundwork for postwar dominance by keeping customers interested and informed when there were no new Cadillacs to buy.

The survival of the dealer network during wartime was one of the keys to Cadillac's post-war dominance of the luxury market. Without new cars to sell, dealers had to turn significant profits in other areas to weather these stormy years. Servicing late model Cadillacs and selling their owners accessories were the primary venues for this. General Motors knew that it was vital for their clients to be involved in the company's war effort. GM's military production publications kept owners informed about Cadillac's tank and aircraft production. With a little luck, the pump would be primed for pre-war buyers to return to showrooms as soon as peace was restored.

Chapter 6 Notes

[108] McCall, 257.

[109] Cadillac Motor Car Division, *Cadillac and Cadillac Fleetwood for 1942* (Detroit, Michigan: Service Department, Cadillac Motor Car Division, 1941),3.

[110] Schneider, *Cadillacs of the Forties,* 76-77.

[111] Lee Kennett, *For the Duration: The United States Goes to War, Pearl Harbor-1942* (New York: Charles Scribner's Sons, 1985. Kennett), 103.

[112] Automobile Manufacturers Association, *Freedom's Arsenal: the story of the Automotive Council for War Production* (Detroit: The Automobile Manufacturers Association, 1950), 60.

[113] "Recooked Autos?" *Business Week,* 25 October 1941, 67.

[114] The New Jersey Zinc Company, "Zinc in Defense," Business Week, 29 November 1941, 9.

[115] Automobile Manufacturers Association, 60.

[116] "Auto Shutdown?" *Business Week,* 7 December 1941, 19.

[117] "No 'Bright Work," *Business Week, 1* November 1941, 16-17.

[118] "Auto trim change," *Business Week*, 29 November 1941, 17-18.

[119] "Car-less Dealers?" *Business Week,* 7 December 1941, 20.

[120] Schneider, *Cadillacs of the Forties,* 76-77.

[121] "Autos to Tanks," *Business Week,* 15 November 1941, 17-18.

[122] "Cars on the skids," *Business Week*, 27 June, 1942, 64.

[123] "Car-less Dealers?" *Business Week,* 7 December 1941, 20.

[124] "Retreader's Boom" *Business Week,* 7 December 1941, 26.

[125] "Lower Octane Fuels," *Cadillac Serviceman,* January-February 1942, 6.

"Actual Need Only Sound Basis for Parts Sales," *Cadillac Serviceman,* March-April 1942, 8.

"Proper Procedure for storage of new Cars is required to Provide Maximum Protection," *Cadillac Serviceman,* March-April 1942, 9,11.

"Thorough Inspection is keynote to longer Car Life," *Cadillac Serviceman,* July-August 1942, 17-18.

"1942 Service Price Book Now Meets OPA Regulations," *Cadillac Serviceman,* July-August 1942, 20.

"Break a Tool, Jap's Delight," *Cadillac Serviceman,* September-October 1942, 22.

[126] "Scrap is Ammunition," *Cadillac Serviceman,* January-February 1943, 2.

"W.P.B. Announces New Drive to Build Scrap Reserve," *Cadillac Serviceman,* September-October 1943, 19.

[127] "Steel needed," *Cadillac Serviceman,* July-August 1943, 14.

"Cadillac Servicemen Play an Important Role in Maintaining Owner Goodwill at High Level," *Cadillac Serviceman,* November-December 1943, 21.

[128] "Most Cadillac Accessories Still Available at Factory," *Cadillac Serviceman,* July-August 1942, 18.

[129] "Newly Developed Cadillac Wheel Locks Prevent Theft of Tires and Wheels," *Cadillac Serviceman,* July-August 1942, 12.

[130] "Cadillac Victory Sweepstakes," *Cadillac Serviceman,* September-October 1943, 17-18.

[131] "Cadillac Mileage Extension Plan," *Cadillac Serviceman,* March- April 1942, 7,9.

[132] Customer Research Staff, General Motors Corporation, *The Automobile User's Guide with Wartime Suggestions* (Detroit, Michigan: General Motors Corporation, 1944), 1.

[133] Cadillac Motor Car Division, *Cadillac...From Peace to War* (Detroit, Michigan: Service Department, Cadillac Motor Car Division, 1944), 6

Illustrated is the Touring Sedan for Five Passengers."

Presenting A NEW *Cadillac-Fleetwood*

AT A MUCH LOWER PRICE !

THE CAR PICTURED HERE—the new Cadillac-Fleetwood Seventy-Two—has every attribute of the most luxurious motor cars ever built—unusual room, rich appointments, and true distinction. Yet it is priced at an unusually moderate figure.

This superb new motor car is a wholly new conception—designed to bring the exclusive advantages of Fleetwood coachcraft to a wider group of people. It is available with standard body designs yet so numerous are the combi-

nations of upholstery, color, and trim that it can be remarkably individualized.

It is equally suited for chauffeur or owner driving. In fact, it is so nimble and quick and easy to handle that it is highly suited to individual transportation.

For the family that wants an all-purpose car —equally proper for the formal occasion or for general usage—the new Cadillac-Fleetwood Seventy-Two is without a rival. We suggest quick action if you need early delivery.

THE NEW

Seventy-Two

$2670 AND UP *delivered at Detroit. Transportation based on rail rates, state and local taxes (if any), optional equipment and accessories—extra. Prices subject to change without notice. White sidewall tires, as shown above, are extra.*

1940 Cadillac Series 72
"Presenting a New Cadillac-Fleetwood at a much lower price!"

1941 Cadillac Series 61 coupe

"You can have everything...including automatic gearshifting!"

1942 Cadillac Series 75 sedan
"Cadillac Fleetwood presents America's most distinguished
motor cars"

AGAIN—THE FINEST CAN BE YOURS!

LOOKING AHEAD—wouldn't you rather have a Cadillac to see you through the months and miles? Wouldn't you rather put your trust in Cadillac's advanced design and uncompromising quality?

You can! You can look forward to almost endless trouble-free miles behind Cadillac's mightiest V-8 engine. You can contemplate years of restful riding in the most comfortable interiors ever created by Fleetwood. *You can do it because again there's a Cadillac at a low price.*

Compare it with any other car. Ask owners what Cadillac's matchless engineering does for stamina and long-range economy. Then let your foresight tell you why, this year, more than ever, *it's wise to buy the best.*

CADILLAC'S THIRD YEAR OF DEFENSE PRODUCTION. Selected in 1939 to make parts for Allison airplane engines, Cadillac has consistently exceeded production schedules.

40ᵀᴴ ANNIVERSARY *CADILLAC*

1942 Cadillac
"Again- The finest can be <u>yours!</u>"

1942 Cadillac Series 61 coupe-
"Again- you can thriftily come up to Cadillac!"

1941 Cadillac Series 61 coupe
"Announcing the new Cadillac-engineered Hydra-matic Drive"

"In training" for twenty-seven years !

When the Japs tried to knock us out at Pearl Harbor—here is one piece of equipment that was ready and waiting for adaptation by the U. S. Army.

It is the Cadillac V-type engine, used by the Army to power its M-5 Light Tank and its tremendous M-8 Howitzer Motor Carriage.

Cadillac V-type engines had gone through twenty-seven years of intensive "training" *before*

Pearl Harbor. There was no question about how they would perform—because they had already passed every civilian test to which a power plant of their type could be subjected. There was no question, either, about how they could "take it."

Adapted by the Army, in combination with Cadillac's Hydra-Matic Transmission, those great V-type engines are giving to tanks a degree

Since 1930, Cadillac has also been producing super-precision assemblies for the Allison America's foremost liquid-cooled aircraft engine.

of mobility—and maneuverability—wholly new in mechanized warfare.

Naturally, these power plants are even better today than when they went into the war; for, with the cooperation of army technicians, our engine research is going consistently ahead.

Every Sunday Afternoon . . . GENERAL MOTORS SYMPHONY OF THE AIR—NBC Network

CADILLAC MOTOR CAR DIVISION   GENERAL MOTORS CORPORATION

LET'S ALL
BACK THE ATTACK
BUY WAR BONDS

Cadillac V-8 engine
"In training for twenty-seven years!"

Cadillac emblem
"We have the <u>right job</u> to do!"

It came out *Fighting!*

When American troops joined in to rid North Africa of its Nazi hordes, they were supported by the new M-5, an all-welded, light tank designed and built by Cadillac, in cooperation with U. S. Army engineers. Observers commenting on its appearance at the front said—"It came out fighting!"

Two Cadillac innovations—wholly new to mechanized warfare—endow the M-5 with speed and maneuverability demoralizing to the enemy. They are innovations which date back to peace—innovations that in other years contributed much to Cadillac's outstanding leadership among fine motor cars.

This departure from conventional tank design called for high confidence in Cadillac's peace-time engineering. But faith in building the M-5 around proved automotive units has been well justified. Exhaustive Army tests, both in and out of battle, have shown that the M-5 can decisively outperform light tanks not possessing its inherent advantages.

We are deeply grateful to the Ordnance Department for its encouragement and co-operation in developing this new light tank. We take pride in the knowledge that production of the M-5 and precision parts for America's most famous liquid-cooled aircraft engine are direct contributions to the Victory that must be ours.

CADILLAC MOTOR CAR DIVISION  GENERAL MOTORS CORPORATION

M-5
"It came out fighting

Making its mark..on a Nazi Mark IV

OUTMANEUVERED at every turn by the harrying tactics of a squadron of high speed American M-5 light tanks, this formidable Nazi Mark IV tank has been immobilized by a well placed hit in its vital mechanism.

The M-5 has been in production at the Cadillac Motor Car Division for over a year. But so perfectly was this military secret kept that few outside Cadillac plants knew of its existence before it swept into battle.

Army Ordnance engineers, familiar with every phase of tank operation, joined forces with Cadillac engineers in developing the M-5. As a result, the M-5 incorporates all that is latest and best in light tank practice plus two innovations from Cadillac peacetime engineering. This accounts for its high speed and great maneuverability.

Likewise entrusted to us are more than 170 vital parts manufactured to extremely close tolerances for America's foremost liquid-cooled aircraft engine. These and other assignments on which Cadillac craftsmen are engaged to the fullest production capacity in our history are war production jobs which take full advantage of all that the Cadillac reputation and tradition imply.

CADILLAC MOTOR CAR DIVISION · GENERAL MOTORS CORPORATION

M-5
"Making its mark..on a Nazi Mark IV"

Commando of the Tanks

Great speed and unequalled maneuverability make the M-5 light tank, built by Cadillac, the commando of the tanks. Commando-like, it strikes swiftly and surely with unfaltering pace wherever it can gain a foothold. Army Ordnance engineers, familiar with every phase of tank operation and the relative success of each type in action, joined forces with Cadillac engineers in developing the M-5. As a result, the M-5 incorporates all that is latest and best in light tank practice plus two innovations from Cadillac peacetime engineering. This accounts for its high speed and great maneuverability. Surrounded by the utmost secrecy, the M-5 had been in full production for more than a year before this phase of Cadillac's war production program became known. Hence it started hitting the enemy with demoralizing results before its existence was suspected. Thus Cadillac's forty years of "know how" is being most effectively used in the service of the nation. Other projects entrusted to us include precision-built inner assemblies for America's foremost liquid-cooled aircraft engine, as well as many other vital parts for the Army and Navy. All of these are products of the type upon which the Cadillac reputation and tradition are founded.

CADILLAC MOTOR CAR DIVISION  GENERAL MOTORS CORPORATION

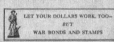

LET YOUR DOLLARS WORK, TOO—
BUY
WAR BONDS AND STAMPS

M-5
"Commando of the Tanks"

Cannon on a rampage... at 30 miles an hour!

Here's a picture of something that the enemy doesn't like! It's a 75-millimeter cannon—roaring along at thirty miles an hour—maneuvering for position from which to pour its high-explosive shells on a moving target.

Utilizing a Cadillac-built tank chassis—which is powered by two Cadillac V-type engines with Hydra-Matic transmissions—this M-8 Howitzer gives to demolition artil-

lery a degree of mobility it has never known before. For the M-8 is not only *fast*—it is highly maneuverable as well.

This is but one of the weapons Cadillac has built for the Allied arsenal. Cadillac also helped to design the M-5 light tank—and produced it in quantity. And, for more than five years, Cadillac has built, in great volume, many precision parts for the Allison engine.

"Victory is our business" here at Cadillac. In 1939 we began working in co-operation with Army Engineers on our first wartime assignment. And since that time we have labored night and day to help give the world's finest fighting men the world's finest armament.

Every Sunday Afternoon . . . GENERAL MOTORS SYMPHONY OF THE AIR—NBC Network

CADILLAC MOTOR CAR DIVISION ★ GENERAL MOTORS CORPORATION

LET'S ALL
BACK THE ATTACK
BUY WAR BONDS

M-8
"Cannon on a rampage... at 30 miles and hour!"

Preview of Cadillac Power

If you were to watch the new M-24 wide-tread tank in action—watch it tear its way through heartbreaking mud and over all kinds of difficult terrain—you would surely conclude that it had some specially-designed, heavy-duty motive power.

But like its predecessors—the M-5 light tank and the M-8 Howitzer Motor Carriage —this new Cadillac-built weapon is powered by two Cadillac V-type engines, driving through Cadillac Hydra-Matic transmissions.

Fundamentally, these are the same famous engines and transmissions that had piled up millions of miles of service in passenger cars long before Cadillac and U. S. Army Ordnance Engineers adapted them to tank design. However, they have been vastly improved as a result of their hard usage on the battlefield.

We doubt whether any other power units originally designed for passenger car use have ever been put to such a gruelling test. We feel sure they will prove a revelation when peace returns.

Every Sunday Afternoon . . . GENERAL MOTORS SYMPHONY OF THE AIR—NBC Network

CADILLAC MOTOR CAR DIVISION  GENERAL MOTORS CORPORATION

LET'S ALL
BACK THE ATTACK
BUY WAR BONDS

M-24
"Preview of Cadillac Power"

Craftsmanship is still our stock in trade

The rhythmic roar of the P-38 tells more eloquently than words of the superb fighting qualities built into its two perfectly synchronized engines. Foremost of the American designed and built liquid-cooled aircraft engines is the Allison, which powers several of our top fighter craft and for which we at Cadillac produce vital precision assemblies.

It was natural that Cadillac should be entrusted with this war production assignment,

because for forty years Cadillac has exemplified the ultimate in craftsmanship and precision. The long-remembered Cadillac motto, "Craftsmanship a Creed—Accuracy a Law," is far from being an empty, meaningless phrase. It is, in fact, the very credo by which we live because it calls for the fullest exercise of our highest traditional skill.

Another assignment is the production of M-5 light tanks, for which the Cadillac automotive-

type V-8 engines were adapted. This serves to keep the same Cadillac craftsmen on the same production line on which they worked in time of peace.

Thus, while serving the nation at war on a full-time basis, we are also maintaining at an efficient peak everything that the Cadillac name and crest represent in time of peace—the peace which must ultimately be ours.

CADILLAC MOTOR CAR DIVISION   GENERAL MOTORS CORPORATION

Lockheed P-38 Lightning
"Craftsmanship is still our stock in trade"

Our <u>fourth</u> year.."*in the Army*"

When war clouds over Europe cast their first long shadows on the American continent, industry was called upon to help speed the armament program, and Cadillac "enlisted." That was back in March of 1939.

Our first assignment was to build vital precision parts for the Allison—America's foremost liquid-cooled aircraft engine—and we've been at it ever since. Today we are producing such important units as the crankshaft, the camshaft, the connecting rods, the reduction gears, the piston pins, and in addition, more than 170 other vital parts for the power train. The parts we make embody some of the finest precision work achieved by American industry. In many instances it calls for tolerances as close as three ten/thousandths of an inch.

But that is not the full story of what Cadillac is doing. We also build the new high-speed M-5 light tank containing two Cadillac-inspired innovations entirely new to mechanized warfare. They were adapted to tank use by U. S. Army ordnance engineers co-operating with Cadillac engineers. This M-5 light tank has been in volume production on Cadillac assembly lines for many months.

We are not only building to the finest standards we have ever achieved—but we are keeping abreast of every assignment made to us.

CADILLAC MOTOR CAR DIVISION · GENERAL MOTORS CORPORATION

LET YOUR DOLLARS WORK, TOO—
BUY
WAR BONDS AND STAMPS

Bell P-39 Aircobra
"Our fourth year...'in the Army'"

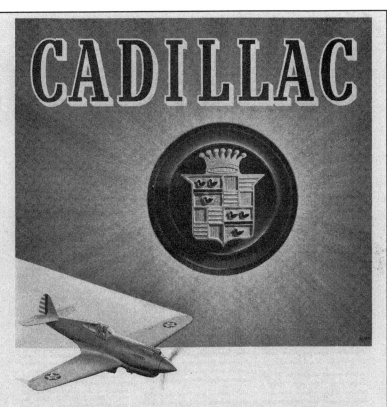

WE'RE STILL WORKING TO CADILLAC STANDARDS !

MUCH of the work we are doing at Cadillac in the great task of arming America is held to limits of accuracy never before achieved in quantity production. . . . The Cadillac-built tanks and the vital precision parts for the famed Allison aircraft engines, which are our special responsibilities today, both demand the very highest order of workmanship and skill. . . . Our work-

men and our shop executives are extremely grateful for these assignments. . . . They enable these superlative craftsmen to turn from the works of peace to the works of war—and still exercise the special skills cultivated over so many years of building to Cadillac standards. . . . In other words, they will continue to be worthy of the Cadillac heritage of quality.

＊　＊　＊　CADILLAC MOTOR CAR DIVISION **GM** GENERAL MOTORS CORPORATION
ARMS FOR VICTORY

AUGUST 1942   83

Curtis P-40 Warhawk
"We're still working to Cadillac Standards"

Arms for America
"Cadillac Style"

SWARMS of planes darkening enemy skies . . . columns of tanks covering conquered earth with their countless numbers—these are the visions which the men and women of Cadillac hold constantly before their eyes. And they are doing their part to make them come true by meeting ever-increasing production schedules for vital parts of a world-famed aircraft engine, and by an ever-mounting production of tanks. But they are still building "Cadillac-style" . . .

still making sure that *quality* walks hand-in-hand with quantity. And these are the results: The precision with which Cadillac builds engine parts adds greatly to fighting plane performance. And Cadillac-built tanks rank among the deadliest offensive weapons in their field. Arms for America—"Cadillac-style"—means armament built to match in quality and potency the skill and courage of America's fighting men—both *Standard of the World.*

CADILLAC MOTOR CAR DIVISION GENERAL MOTORS CORPORATION

Curtis P-40 Warhawk
"Arms for America 'Cadillac Style'"

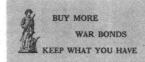

Contemplative Buyer- 1945

"Ther's one thing he's sure about..."

Cadillac

"I know what I'll buy *first!*"

High on the postwar purchasing list of most Cadillac owners is another Cadillac car.

No other car in America—according to a nation-wide survey—has such a firm hold on the loyalty of its owners.

Three million motorists were recently asked to express an opinion as to what make they expected their next car to be. And those who own Cadillacs led the owners of all makes in saying

they intended to "repeat" on their present cars.

This, of course, is but logical. Wartime driving has made it clearer than ever that Cadillac quality stands alone. Cadillac's beauty and comfort and safety have always been factors which the buyer could see and appraise—but only extended usage can reveal the full value of Cadillac craftsmanship. The years and the miles are unusually kind to a Cadillac.

In the future, as in the past, Cadillac cars will be built in the Cadillac tradition—where craftsmanship is a creed, and accuracy a law. There will be but a single Cadillac standard—and that the "Standard of the World."

Every Sunday Afternoon . . . GENERAL MOTORS SYMPHONY ON THE AIR—NBC Network

CADILLAC MOTOR CAR DIVISION — GENERAL MOTORS CORPORATION

BUY MORE

WAR BONDS

KEEP WHAT YOU HAVE

Contemplative Buyer
"I know what I'll buy first!"- 1945

Part III

Cadillac Goes To War: Military Production

Tanks did not start rolling off Cadillac's assembly lines in early 1942 without serious prior planning. *Business Week* reported a year before Pearl Harbor that General Motors had taken on $410,400,00 worth of defense work. The largest portion of that total involved Cadillac. Allison aircraft engines accounted for $164,800,000 of the total. Cadillac produced numerous internal parts for these engines.[134] The M-5 contract would follow in 1941.[135]

Cadillac made significant contributions to the war in the air. Allison aircraft engines powered Allied warplanes from the sands of the Sahara to the frozen wastes of the Aleutians. With Cadillac's reputation for quality, there was no question who would produce a variety of internal parts for Allison's powerful V-1710 liquid cooled engine.

Chapter 7

Clark Avenue at war 1942-1945

In May 1938, the Curtis P-40 was chosen as the Army Air Corps' primary single engine fighter. They were to be powered by the Allison V-1710, a twelve cylinder "v" style liquid-cooled engine. The government ordered eight hundred engines for these new aircraft. Cadillac was contracted in 1939 to produce camshafts, connecting rods, piston pins, and reduction gear for the V-1710. The following July, Cadillac was recruited to redesign the crankshaft and blower gear drives for the two-stage supercharger. The Cadillac-built parts helped increase the Allison engine's output by forty percent.[136] The V-1710 was used by a myriad of aircraft, from the P-38 Lightning, P-39 Airacobra, P-40 Warhawk, to the early series P-51 Mustangs. Over 70,000 engines were supplied to the Army Air Force from 1939 to 1947.[137]

Cadillac Servicemen go to war

The Second World War was the first truly mechanized war. For every four soldiers, six mechanics and technicians were needed by the U.S. military.[138] Producing 15,000 tanks and parts for 70,000 aircraft engines created a problem for Cadillac and the rest of General Motors. Someone had to service their products once they left the factory. To fill this need, GM created the War Service Program under the direction of Vice President of Engineering C.L. McCuen. Three points within the program insured that the company's products would survive the war.

Under the first point, GM prepared mechanics to service tanks and aircraft. These technicians were trained in four different types of operations. The first group learned to service the equipment in the field. The second group was comprised of field mechanics who worked in light maintenance facilities. A third group labored in semi-mobile repair shops doing major repairs. The final group worked in overhaul shops.

The second point involved experienced General Motors employees. GM engineers were placed in the field to observe the performance under wartime conditions and suggest changes that would improve serviceability. Under the third point, GM made sure that both the army and navy had sufficient spare parts to keep their weapons functioning. The cost of the War Service Program was projected to exceed $5,000,000 the first year.[139]

By January 1943, General Motors' sixteen schools were turning out 2,000 technicians monthly. Experienced mechanics needed as little as ten days to become proficient at their new duties, while others required up to eleven weeks of training. Nearly a quarter of these men graduated from Allison's engine school, making them skilled aircraft mechanics. Others learned to work under the pressure of combat. Most were trained as gas or diesel mechanics to service the vast number of vehicles in Army, Navy, and Marine inventories, including the Cadillac built M-5, M-8, M-19, and M-24 tanks.[140]

The M-3

The success of the Wehrmacht's panzer divisions undoubtedly prompted a tremendous expenditure on the U.S. Army's tank arsenal. There was a difference in philosophy between the U.S Army and its German counterpart. American planners insisted that tanks be light and fast, weighing between ten and twenty tons. German tanks typically were slower and four times heavier, but were better armored. As late as August 1940, the only producers of tanks in the United States were American Car and Foundry, Baldwin Locomotive, and American Locomotive. Their contracts for light, medium, and heavy tanks amounted to $121,000,000.[141] General Motors, Ford, and Chrysler did not seriously begin discussing production goals of 2,500 tanks monthly until November 1941. These contracts amounted to $39,000,000 for Ford and $25,782,000 for GM's Flint, Michigan plants. Fisher Body Plant #1 in Flint, with 45,000 employees, would be the center of General Motors' tank production.[142]

In 1940, a new medium tank was ordered by the U.S. Army, the M-3. It was tested for the press at Aberdeen Proving Ground in April 1941, where the tank decimated the older armored vehicles pitted against it. The cast steel hull was widely praised as more rugged than the earlier riveted type.[143] The primary advantage of the new style hull was that shell impacts would not dislodge rivets and turn them into projectiles, dramatically improving crew survivability. American Locomotive Company was the sole producer of the improved M-3A1 in late 1941.[144]

In early 1941, it appeared that the M-3 Grant/Lee would be the workhorse of U.S. Army armored divisions in the upcoming conflict. Several problems seemed to be likely to prevent delivery in large numbers. While the improved M-3A1 was built at American Locomotive, the older style riveted hull versions were made only at one Baldwin Locomotive plant. At least six new plants were needed to supply the current version to the U.S. Army. The first of these Baldwin plants was built in sixty one days, between June 18 and August 19, 1941.[145] While that solved one problem in the short term, a much larger problem loomed.

The M-3 was powered by a single aircraft style radial engine. Several drawbacks were quite obvious with this setup. As an air-cooled engine, the radial generated a lot of heat, and required a great deal of airflow to function properly. Aircraft engines also typically required 100 octane aviation fuel. If a way could be found to run tanks on lower octane automotive gas, the better fuel could then be allocated to the Army Air Force. None of the engine designs available at Ford or Chrysler produced sufficient power to move a tank.[146] In the spring of 1941, engineers at Cadillac arrived at a solution.

M-5 tank development

Cadillac replaced an M-3's radial engine with a pair of automotive V-8s, one driving each track. The prototype was maneuvered by manipulating dual throttle levers. The Army's Ordinance Department was duly impressed with the hybrid tank's performance. It started easily, was very agile, and was very smooth at low speed.[147] Much of this was attributed to the Hydra-Matic transmission bolted to each engine. War Department officials were so impressed with the performance of the new tanks that they placed an order for 75 units in November 1941. Less than six months later, the M-5 was in full production at Cadillac.[148]

Cadillac's current design V-8 engine had been in production since 1936 and would continue to see service until 1948. By 1941, it displaced 346 cubic inches and produced 150 brake horsepower, of which 39.2 horses were taxable. The former figure denoted the energy produced by the engine without the transmission, fan, water pump, generator, or any belts attached. The latter shows how much of that power could be used when the engine was installed in a car. The pistons were aluminum with two compression rings and two oil rings.[149] Since March 1941, it had been coupled with the four speed fully automatic Hydra-Matic transmission. It was a hydro-mechanical unit, with shifting controlled by fluid pressure. Unlike later transmissions, it did not need a vacuum assist, or did it require cooling via the radiator.[150] To modern eyes, the Cadillac powertrain appears to be somewhat crude. For its day, it was one of the most reliable combinations available.

The 346 and Hydra-Matic in Military Guise

In order to meet the demands of military use, the engine and transmission were modified extensively. Overhaul periods for tanks usually occurred at 400 hours or 4,000 miles, due to the extreme conditions under which they labored. Molybdenum, a heat resistant metal, was added to the cast iron engine blocks to increase fatigue resistance. A drain slot was added to the rear main bearing to reduce oil seal leakage while operating on inclines. Durex bearings were used for longer life. To reduce detonation failures due to poor fuel, cast iron three ring pistons replaced the lighter four ring civilian ones, and new flanges were added to the head gaskets. The rings on the pistons were chrome plated to reduce wear in the cylinder bores. To allow for operation on sixty degree slopes, the oil sump depth was increased to prevent a loss of oil pressure, and the carburetor floats were redesigned to keep the engine from suffering from fuel starvation. The 24 volt electrical system required much heavier generators. To support the extra weight, the engine front cover was strengthened. To assist in keeping water and electricity flowing under combat conditions, a triple belt system was used in lieu of the civilian two belt setup. Valves and valve guides were hardened to improve durability. To prevent vapor lock at high operating temperatures, the fuel pump was relocated from the front of the engine to the fuel tank.[151] For easier servicing, the oil dipstick was shifted from a boss on the left side of the engine block to ports on either side of the oil pan.

The Hydra-Matic transmission underwent a few modifications as well. In the M-5, a pair of Cadillac drive trains sat backwards in the aft compartment of the tank with individual propeller shafts running to a common transfer case near the front of the vehicle. Thanks to this two speed transfer case, the M-5 now had six speeds forward and in reverse gear. An oil cooler was added to cool the transmission fluid. In civilian application, the transmission is fairly exposed, allowing the heat generated by shifting to dissipate. There was very little air circulation within a tank hull, so this new method was required. Steel alloy screws were used to attach the flywheel cover to prevent oil loss. The pins holding planetary gears were also nitrided for greater durability.[152]

The reliability of the Cadillac drivetrain in the M-5 was tested in the harshest climates available stateside, exposing it to heat, cold, dust, and rugged terrain. The engine was subjected to stresses that its designers could not have imagined, operating at 4250 to 5000 rpm.[153] The powerplant was considered to be almost indestructible. No power was lost during shifting and the engine could not be over-revved. Not surprisingly, it passed with flying colors.[154] While the M-5 could operate with one engine damaged, the remaining engine was barely capable of moving the tank out of immediate danger. Still, a crippled twin engine M-5 might remain mobile when a single engine M-3 would be completely inoperable. This allowed for a greater likelihood that a damaged M-5 could be repaired and sent back into battle, while the M-3 would have to be abandoned.

The M-5 went on to serve in North Africa and Italy. It was light and fast, but took heavy losses due to its thin armor. However, part of American strategy was to use massed forces to overcome these deficiencies. To fill the need, Cadillac stepped up production, creating 300 M-5s per month in 1942.[155] After Fortress Europe was breached on June 6, 1944, tank losses required immediate replacement. M-5 production was farmed out to Massey-Harris in Racine, Wisconsin, and to American Car and Foundry in Berwick, Pennsylvania and Saint Charles, Missouri. The latter company was charged with repairing an additional 1,200 M-5 and M-3 tanks.[156] Battle damaged M-5s were shipped to Evansville, Indiana, where Chrysler employees repaired and upgraded 2,000 units in mid-1944.[157]

Later Developments

In December 1944, Cadillac engineers W.G. Pierce, A. Majewski, F. Burrell, and W. Voight issued a proposal to the company entitled "High Output Tank Engine Development." They noted in the report that the output of the current Cadillac tank engine might be improved significantly if even more significant internal changes were made. Quietness and a smooth idle, though highly prized in luxury cars, were of little use in combat. The engineers posited that sacrifices in these areas would produce a more powerful tank engine. $35,600 was budgeted to experiment with improved valves, dual carburetion and exhaust, new fans, and redesigned camshafts. These changes resulted in engines that produced thirty-four more horsepower than the previous tank engine.[158] The end of the war halted the development of this engine, but the lessons learned were soon applied to post war engines.

Over 15,000 Cadillac powered armored vehicles were constructed between March 1942 and August 1945. A new light tank, the M-24 Chaffee, went into production in April 1944.[159] The new tank was a vast improvement over the M-5. While the earlier vehicle weighed in at thirteen tons and was armed with a thirty-seven millimeter cannon, its successor was a considerably heftier at 18 tons and packed a much larger punch with its seventy-five millimeter main gun. The M-8 was a motorized howitzer mounted on an M-5 chassis. In 1945, the M-19 joined the M-24 rumbling down Clark Avenue's line. This new vehicle consisted of a pair of forty millimeter anti-aircraft guns mounted atop an M-24 hull. The last M-24 rolled off the assembly line on August 24, 1945, signaling that civilian production was not too far in the future.[160]

Chapter 7 notes

[134] "GM Defense Job: armament program's impact on American Industry," *Business Week,* 14 December 1940, 28.

[135] Maurice D. Hendry, *Cadillac: Standard of the World: The Complete 70 Year History* (Princeton, New Jersey: Princeton Publishing, 1973), 240.

[136] Arch Brown, "Cadillac- A Complete History, Part VIII: In wartime and beyond," *Cars and Parts,* August 1991, 40.

[137] Hendry, *Cadillac: Standard of the World: The Complete 70 Year History,* 240-243.

[138] "How industry is training war mechanics," *Newsweek,* 23 November 1942, 54.

[139] "GM War Service Program," *Aviation,* May 1942, 190.

[140] "Training speeded: military need for repair and maintenance specialists spurs GM output to over 2000 trainees a month," *Business Week,* 16 January, 1943, 74.

[141] "Tanks: Coming up," *Business Week,* 17 May 1941, 22.

[142] "Autos to Tanks," 17-18.

[143] "M3: The army's newest tank," *Time,* 14 April 1941, 22-23.

[144] "First Cast Steel Tank" *Business Week,* 7 December 1941, 17.

[145] "Heavy Tank Armor," *Business Week,* 18 October 1941, 18-19.

[146] Doug Houston, "The Role of Classic engines in World War II," *The Classic Car,* July 2005, 18-19.

[147] Hendry, *Cadillac: Standard of the World: The Complete 70 Year History,* 240.

[148] Brown, "Cadillac- A Complete History, Part VIII," 41.

[149] *Cadillac and Cadillac Fleetwood for 1941,* back cover.

[150] Cadillac Motor Car Division, *Cadillac Shop Manual for 1942* (Detroit, Michigan: Service Department, Cadillac Motor Car Division, 1941), 80-82.

[151] John F. Gordon, Chief Engineer, Cadillac Motor Car Division, 1945, "Cadillac Twin V-8 Power Plant for Light Tanks," *The Self Starter,* Fall 1992, 9,13,15.

[152] Ibid., 15.

[153] Ibid., 14.

[154] "V-8 for victory: Ford engine for medium tanks as army's choice," *Business Week,* 19 December, 1942, 14.

[155] Schneider, *Cadillacs of the Forties,* 77.

[156] "Back to war job: renewed demand for tanks," *Business Week,* 8 July, 1944, 22-23.

[157] "Repair is stressed in new tank program," *Business Week,* 22 July, 1944, 47.

[158] Jack Hoffman, "The High Output Cadillac Tank Engine Program," *The Self Starter,* October 1999, 18-20.

[159] Schneider, *Cadillacs of the Forties,* 77.

[160] McCall, 262-263.

Chapter 8

Consumer attitude adjustment 1942-1945

No evidence has yet surfaced showing that the federal government explicitly controlled the content of private sector ads during the war. However, Lizabeth Cohen's *A Consumer's Republic* noted that the proper regulation of consumer behavior fit into war needs. Period literature attempted to make some buying patterns more patriotic than others. Following rationing regulations, paying no more than recommended price for scarce items, and planting Victory Gardens were all praised as being helpful to the war effort. The practitioners were dubbed "citizen consumers."[161] There were, however, less scrupulous Americans who hoarded prized goods or participated in the black market. These "purchaser consumers" were therefore deemed unpatriotic because they placed their own needs above those of the nation.[162]

Wartime print advertising was directed at encouraging the behavior of the citizen consumer while repressing that of the purchaser consumer. In ads, the American way of life, in the guise of limitless bounties of consumer goods, was the true reason for bringing the war to a swift conclusion. This served a multitude of purposes. People were encouraged to invest in savings and war bonds as a means of saving for future big ticket purchases. Inflation was curbed in this manner. Additionally, the promotion of consumer goods during a period when none were available primed the pump for immediate post war consumption, hopefully staving off a recession like the one that followed World War I.[163] Advertising continued on this theme for a short time after the war. A Texaco ad titled "Wanted...more miracles!" showed a couple carrying a bounty of consumer goods including a car, a house, a steam iron, and a sewing machine. The copy noted that American industry had produced everything the country needed during the war, and post war consumers wanted the same consideration.[164] Some of the ideas mentioned in Cohen's book were played out by Cadillac's ad writers during World War II.

Cadillac Wartime Print Advertising

It makes good sense to keep customers aware of their favorite manufacturer's wartime activities. Keeping one's name in front of the public would help maintain interest until civilian production was resumed. Wartime advertising fell into five basic categories: automobile, abstract, aircraft, armor, and contemplative customer. New Cadillacs were in production for nearly two months after Pearl Harbor. Even before the outbreak of hostilities, ad writers were getting the jitters. In "Again- The Finest Can Be <u>Yours</u>," While touting the durability of their cars, the ad bluntly stated, "...this year, more than ever, it's wise to buy the best."[165] A similar sentiment was expressed in "Again- You Can <u>Thriftily</u> Come Up to Cadillac." Both ads show the new 1942 Cadillac, but the lower left hand corner of each is dedicated to Allison V-1710 powered fighters.[166] Interestingly, "True to a Long Tradition," an ad printed for Series 75 cars, mentioned defense production and the impending war with the almost unnoticeable line at the bottom of the page, "3rd Year of Defense Production."[167] Perhaps Cadillac wanted to keep its wealthiest clients free from worry.

The second category of ad was a little more abstract. "We have the <u>right job</u> to do" featured a cannon firing across a Cadillac crest.

"Only the products are different" appeared in *Life* on November 9, 1942, about the time M-5s were getting their first taste of combat in American hands. This ad featured a crest with a small P-39 in the corner. It assured the reader that "We're still adapting precision workmanship to the requirements of quantity production- precisely the type of endeavor for which we've trained for the past forty years." [168]

The exploits of the Flying Tigers in the skies over China during the opening months of the war convinced Cadillac to focus on the Allison powered P-40 Warhawk in several ads. "We're still working to Cadillac Standards," appearing in the August 1942 issue of *Motor*, featured one of these fighters streaking by a Cadillac crest.[169] "We've put 44 million man-hours in the air" showed a P-40 with its engine drawn as a cutaway. Appearing in *Newsweek* on January 24, 1944, the fighter was being relegated to secondary roles to make way for newer aircraft, but the mystique of the early months of the war remained.[170]

The P-38 found plenty of exposure as well. One was seen escorting a wave of B-17s across the pages of *Life* as the heavy bombers pounded a Japanese city in "Pay-off for Pearl Harbor."[171] The Luftwaffe did not escape Cadillac's wrath. "Craftsmanship is still our stock in trade" showed a P-38 sporting mid-war red fringed insignia dispatching what appears to be an Me-110.[172] The P-39 did not rate many ads to itself, perhaps due to its less impressive combat record in American hands. "Our fourth year..' in the army" is a rare example, showing a flight of P-39s preparing for takeoff.[173] However, small P-39s appear in the corner of many ads to represent all Cadillac V-1710 production. Early model P-51s were roaring down the runway, no doubt on their way to intercept a squadron of Japanese bombers, in "Forty years of 'know how' in its nose," printed in *Newsweek* on May 31, 1943.[174]

The M-5 was the most popular subject of Cadillac's wartime ads. "We're doing the job we're best fitted to do!" appeared in *Life* on October 19, 1942.[175] "It came out fighting," "Commando of the tanks," "Making its mark..on a Nazi Mark IV," "Cadillac's own V for Victory," "It's performance is a Peacetime Triumph," all appeared in 1943 to extol the virtues of Cadillac quality in M-5 production.[176] For 1944, the spotlight had to be shared with a newcomer, the M-8 motorized howitzer. "Cannon on a rampage... at 30 miles an hour!" featured the M-8 careening over rough terrain while blasting an enemy position with its huge seventy-five millimeter mortar.[177] "Some go through- some go over!" showed an M-5 splashing across a river while the M-8 rides atop a pontoon bridge.[178] A trainload of M-5s shared the spotlight with a flight of P-38s in "No wonder the Japs are amazed!" The ad noted that:

> The Japs are reported to have confessed their amazement at America's ability to arm herself. They could not comprehend the ability of a free country to convert its vast facilities to war production in so short a time.[179]

A disembodied 346 and Hydra-Matic appeared in front of a trio of M-5s in the July 24, 1944 issue of *Time*, proclaiming that that driveline had been "In training for twenty-seven years!"[180] It is interesting to note that the artist made no effort to replicate the wartime engine, as the dipstick and fuel pump were clearly in their pre-war locations.

The new M-24 Chaffee was the featured tank for 1945's Cadillac ads. "Peacetime power with a wartime job" and "Imprint of Cadillac Power" appeared in *Life* during the spring.[181] The latter raved about the soundness of the Cadillac design.

> The success of Cadillac V-type engine and Hydra-Matic transmission in powering tanks- the ease with which these power units were adapted to tank use- and their inherent ability to bring a new degree of maneuverability to tank warfare-are all conclusive evidence of their fundamental soundness of design. Abnormal wartime use has subjected both engine and transmission to tests never encountered in civilian use. As a result, they have been improved in many ways. [182]

"Preview of Cadillac Power" foreshadowed the return of peacetime production.

We doubt whether any other power units originally designed for passenger car use have ever been put to such a grueling test. We feel sure that they will prove a revelation when peace returns.[183]

"Famous in peace- distinguished in battle" made similar claims about the improved nature of the Cadillac engine.[184] Cadillac's ad writers were subtly beginning the reconversion process months before any cars would be produced.

The final incarnation of the wartime ad at Cadillac was the "contemplative buyer," a series of ads that ran in the summer of 1945. A distinguished gentleman asserted that "There's one thing he's sure about." His next car would be a Cadillac. The ad noted that in a survey of 3,000,000 car owners, Cadillac had the highest percentage of repeat business.[185] The same survey was touted in "Just waiting for the day," where another distinguished gentleman in a finely upholstered chair is gazing longingly at a Cadillac brochure.[186]

The lady of the house was not left out in these ads. "I know what I'll buy first!" repeated the assertion that Cadillac owners would continue to be loyal to the company even when peace offers other driving options.[187] The armed forces also found a place in this series. The one thing that a general and an admiral found themselves "In complete agreement" on was their shared desire to buy another Cadillac after the war. The ad noted that servicemen who owned Cadillacs or LaSalles before the war were more likely to buy new models after the cessation of hostilities.[188]

Advantage- Cadillac

Cadillac gained a tremendous competitive advantage thanks to its war production. While Packard was busy building PT boat engines and Rolls-Royce Merlin airplane engines, Cadillac was able to continue refining its drivetrain. When the war ended, that would be one less thing for the company to reconvert. Aircraft engineering required much closer tolerances than automotive production. By producing the most vital parts of the V-1710 for

Allison, Cadillac reinforced its image of quality. The airman was the most romanticized warrior of the Second World War. It certainly didn't hurt Cadillac's image when one recalls that the fabled "Flying Tigers" flew P-40s, and that Admiral Yamamoto was shot down by a pair of P-38s, an aircraft also used by America's top two aces. Even the P-39 gained notoriety in the early days of the Pacific War in the Aleutians and on Guadalcanal.[189]

Training mechanics skilled in working on Cadillac engines was helpful in two ways. First, it provided a pool of experienced mechanics from which the company could draw after the war. Secondly, these men were undoubtedly impressed with the quality of the engines that they serviced. Certainly, more than a few bought Cadillac in succeeding years because of their wartime experiences.

The effects of Cadillac's wartime efforts to expand market share were not fully realized until after the war ended and car production resumed. Using war production to improve its engines and transmissions was a brilliant move on Cadillac's part. When civilian production resumed, the company would not be selling warmed over 1942 models. Retooling at Cadillac took less time and was less costly than at Packard or Lincoln. By offering top notch service and selling useful accessories to existing customers, Cadillac made a positive impact on that base. Keeping its customer base informed of the company's wartime activities was useful too, allowing loyal Cadillac customers to feel as if they were a part of the war effort. Advertising reinforced the quality of Cadillac products, even if tanks and airplane engines bore little resemblance to automobiles. If the survey of 3,000,000 car owners had any truth to it, Cadillac's ploy to keep its customers loyal during three and a half years without a single new car in any showroom worked like magic. The key to success in the post war era would lie in capitalizing on these advantages before the competition could regroup and refocus their energies on car production.

Chapter 8 Notes

[161] Lizabeth Cohen, *A Consumers' Republic: The Politics of Mass Consumption in Postwar America (Vintage Books: New York, 2003)*, 67.

[162] Ibid., 69.

[163] Ibid., 70.

[164] Texaco Corporation, "Wanted...more miracles!" *Business Week*, 19 January, 1946, 3.

[165] Cadillac Motor Car Division, "Again- The Finest Can Be Yours," magazine advertisement, 1941, in J.D. Shively Cadillac Literature Collection, Greencastle, Indiana.

[166] Cadillac Motor Car Division, "Again- You Can Thriftily Come Up to Cadillac," magazine advertisement, 1941, in J.D. Shively Cadillac Literature Collection, Greencastle, Indiana.

[167] Cadillac Motor Car Division, "True to a Long Tradition," magazine advertisement, 1941, in J.D. Shively Cadillac Literature Collection, Greencastle, Indiana.

[168] Cadillac Motor Car Division, "We have the right job to do," magazine advertisement, 1942, in J.D. Shively Cadillac Literature Collection, Greencastle, Indiana.

Cadillac Motor Car Division, "Only the products are different," magazine advertisement, 1942, in J.D. Shively Cadillac Literature Collection, Greencastle, Indiana.

[169] Cadillac Motor Car Division, "We're still working to Cadillac Standards," magazine advertisement, 1942, in J.D. Shively Cadillac Literature Collection, Greencastle, Indiana.

[170] Cadillac Motor Car Division, "We've put 44 million man-hours in the air," magazine advertisement, 1944, in J.D. Shively Cadillac Literature Collection, Greencastle, Indiana.

[171] Cadillac Motor Car Division, "Pay-off for Pearl Harbor," magazine advertisement, 1944, in J.D. Shively Cadillac Literature Collection, Greencastle, Indiana.

[172] Cadillac Motor Car Division, "Craftsmanship is still our stock in trade," magazine advertisement, 1943, in J.D. Shively Cadillac Literature Collection, Greencastle, Indiana.

[173] Cadillac Motor Car Division, "Our fourth year..' in the army," magazine advertisement, 1943, in J.D. Shively Cadillac Literature Collection, Greencastle, Indiana.

[174] Cadillac Motor Car Division, "Forty years of 'Know How' in its nose," magazine advertisement, 1943, in J.D. Shively Cadillac Literature Collection, Greencastle, Indiana.

[175] Cadillac Motor Car Division, "We're doing the job we're best fitted to do!" magazine advertisement, 1942, in J.D. Shively Cadillac Literature Collection, Greencastle, Indiana.

[176] Cadillac Motor Car Division, "It came out fighting," magazine advertisement, 1943, in J.D. Shively Cadillac Literature Collection, Greencastle, Indiana.

Cadillac Motor Car Division, "Commando of the tanks," magazine advertisement, 1943, in J.D. Shively Cadillac Literature Collection, Greencastle, Indiana.

Cadillac Motor Car Division, "Making its mark..on a Nazi Mark IV," magazine advertisement, 1943, in J.D. Shively Cadillac Literature Collection, Greencastle, Indiana.

Cadillac Motor Car Division, "Cadillac's own V for Victory," magazine advertisement, 1943, in J.D. Shively Cadillac Literature Collection, Greencastle, Indiana.

Cadillac Motor Car Division, "It's performance is a Peacetime Triumph," magazine advertisement, 1943, in J.D. Shively Cadillac Literature Collection, Greencastle, Indiana.

[177] Cadillac Motor Car Division, "Cannon on a rampage... at 30 miles an hour!" magazine advertisement, 1944, in J.D. Shively Cadillac Literature Collection, Greencastle, Indiana.

[178] Cadillac Motor Car Division, "Some go through- some go over!" magazine advertisement, 1944, in J.D. Shively Cadillac Literature Collection, Greencastle, Indiana.

[179] Cadillac Motor Car Division, "No wonder the Japs are amazed!" magazine advertisement, 1944, in J.D. Shively Cadillac Literature Collection, Greencastle, Indiana.

[180] Cadillac Motor Car Division, "In training for twenty-seven years!" magazine advertisement, 1944, in J.D. Shively Cadillac Literature Collection, Greencastle, Indiana.

181 Cadillac Motor Car Division, "Peacetime power with a wartime job," magazine advertisement, 1945, in J.D. Shively Cadillac Literature Collection, Greencastle, Indiana.

182 Cadillac Motor Car Division, "Imprint of Cadillac Power," magazine advertisement, 1945, in J.D. Shively Cadillac Literature Collection, Greencastle, Indiana.

183 Cadillac Motor Car Division, "Preview of Cadillac Power," magazine advertisement, 1945, in J.D. Shively Cadillac Literature Collection, Greencastle, Indiana.

184 Cadillac Motor Car Division, "Famous in peace- distinguished in battle," magazine advertisement, 1945, in J.D. Shively Cadillac Literature Collection, Greencastle, Indiana.

185 Cadillac Motor Car Division, "There's one thing he's sure about," magazine advertisement, 1945, in J.D. Shively Cadillac Literature Collection, Greencastle, Indiana.

186 Cadillac Motor Car Division, "Just waiting for the day," magazine advertisement, 1945, in J.D. Shively Cadillac Literature Collection, Greencastle, Indiana.

187 Cadillac Motor Car Division, "I know what I'll buy first!" magazine advertisement, 1945, in J.D. Shively Cadillac Literature Collection, Greencastle, Indiana.

188 Cadillac Motor Car Division, "In complete agreement," magazine advertisement, 1945, in J.D. Shively Cadillac Literature Collection, Greencastle, Indiana.

189 John Huston, The War Department, "Report from the Aleutians," motion picture, 1944.

Part IV

Reconversion And Dominace

The tide of war had begun to turn in 1944. Manufacturers could see a light at the end of the tunnel. The prospect of civilian production seemed to be a real possibility in the near future. Although it might be a few years before reconversion, Cadillac intended to lay the groundwork to capitalize on wartime advantages as soon as peace was declared. The company had made great strides toward dominance prior to the war by redefining the meaning of luxury. During the war, Cadillac had been allowed to modernize its facilities and improve its drivetrain at War Department expense, an advantage not granted to Packard. When the war ended, it was only a matter of time before Cadillac would permanently gain the upper hand.

Chapter 9

Packard Sings the Reconversion Blues 1944-1946

It should not be surprising that General Motors, and the rest of the auto industry, had been planning for post war production for quite some time. *Business Week* addressed the issue six months before Pearl Harbor. The author noted that an economic slump, not unlike that of 1919, might occur after the cessation of hostilities. The sudden termination of military contracts would be the likely cause of this downturn. Production capacity was expected to rise during the war. The real challenge was how to utilize this new capacity in a post war world. While a plant designed to build bombers might excel at that task, it was uncertain if these facilities could be converted to automobile production.[190] Those questions had to be answered long before the shooting stopped.

Packard at war

Packard did not have the same wartime production advantages that Cadillac enjoyed, although the situation looked good on paper. In 1943, the company sold $341,000,000 worth of war goods. The following year was even better, with sales of $455,000,000. A record number of employees wore Packard coveralls, standing at 36,000. At the close of hostilities in 1945, the company had cash and securities worth $55,000,000. Viewed purely from a financial angle, Packard was well-equipped for post war combat with Cadillac.[191]

Packard's contribution to the war effort was considerably different than that of Cadillac. Instead of producing the company's fine inline eight cylinder automotive engine, Packard built Merlin V-12 aircraft engines on license from Rolls-Royce. Merlins powered the Spitfires and Hurricanes that defended London during the Blitz, securing a place in the history books. British manufacturers Supermarine and Hawker needed more engines than could be produced domestically, so they sought out other suppliers. Packard readily agreed and eventually produced 43,000 of the engines for British and American use.[192] When the first example arrived in the U.S., engineers were shocked by what they found. The Merlin was a fantastic engine, but it was largely hand built. Major components, such as pistons and crankshafts, didn't interchange between engines. This was a real problem when servicing engines in the far flung reaches of a global conflict. Under combat conditions, the last thing a field mechanic wanted to do was try to machine a rod bearing to fit the particular engine that he was trying to repair. In order to produce the number of engines required, Packard engineers literally redesigned the Merlin from the pan up.[193] The end result was magnificent when fitted to the P-51 Mustang, a marriage that resulted in the finest piston-engine fighter ever produced.

Packard Falters: 1944-1958

While it had entered the history books by building the engine that allowed the P-51 to save the concept of daylight bombing, Packard hadn't done itself any favors with post war production. The pre-war body dies, with the exception of those used in the Clipper, were sold to the Soviet Union during the war at the behest of the War Production Board to help with that nation's post-war conversion to auto production. As a result, Packard had only one set of body dies that would have to be used for the entire 1946-1947 line.[194] Before the first car could be assembled, 200,000 government owned machines and tools had to be removed from the plant. Raw materials and partially finished products amounting to $35,000,000 had to be returned to the government. Over 3,200 pieces of civilian equipment had to be removed from storage and re-installed in the Packard factory. A new final assembly plant had to be added. Steel shortages didn't help matters either. Labor strife hurt Packard worse than Cadillac, as it relied heavily on striking outside suppliers. At the end of 1946, Packard's books showed a combined loss of $7,000,000 from operations, not a very healthy way to start the post war era.[195]

Packard made a potentially fatal miscalculation regarding the future of aviation late in the war. *Business Week* reported in July 1944 that the company intended to continue making updated Merlin engines after the war ended. Packard president George T. Christopher also stated that the company would also produce a version of it popular marine engine as an industrial power plant. These two operations would occupy precious production space, as well as bleed off over twenty percent of the company's work force.[196] The additional floor space and machinery needed for this venture had a $3,500,000 price tag.[197] Defense contracts are generally a good thing, but Packard's timing could not have been worse. The summer of 1944 saw the first combat use of jet aircraft. It is true that the piston powered P-51 would soldier on into the 1950s, but the age of the propeller was rapidly reaching its end.

Packard seemed to many observers to be doing well immediately after World War II. 1949 was its first 100,000 unit sales year.[198]

However, Packard lagged behind Cadillac technologically. The company suffered from tooling issues. Despite the installation of new transfer machines in the engine production line after the war, the net cost reduction for each eight cylinder unit was only seventeen percent. The savings were even less for sixes.[199] Packard lacked an automatic transmission until 1949, nearly a decade after Cadillac. The archaic inline eight soldiered on until 1955, when a V-8 was finally offered.[200] Sales continued to falter, causing more financial troubles for Packard. The following year, Packard president Jim Nance inked a merger deal with Studebaker. There was hopeful news from the aviation division in the early 1950s. The company began building General Electric J47 jet engines under license in 1952. Regrettably, these 3,025 units were of little help in rescuing Packard from its fate.[201]

The final years of the company were unspectacular. The 1958 Packard was little more than a badge engineered Studebaker Hawk. The last Packard rolled down the assembly line on July 13, 1958, an ignominious end for a once proud marque.[202] The company's inability to rapidly and inexpensively reconvert after World War II had eventually destroyed it. The 1950s had not been kind to Packard, but errors during the final years of production should not negate the glories of earlier days. The Packard Twelves of the 1930s and the Darrins of the early 1940s will always remain as high water marks for automotive elegance.

Chapter 9 Notes

[190] "Memo to a post war planner," *Business Week,* 14 June 1941, 84.

[191] Neil Torrence, "Did the Packard Win the War or Was It a Casualty Thereof?" *The Classic Car,* June 1999, 48-49.

[192] Ibid., 48.

[193] Enzo Angelucci, *The Rand McNally Encyclopedia of Military Aircraft, 1914-1980* (New York: The Military Press, 1977), 233-234.

[194] Jim Donnelly, "Powering to victory: The revolutionary wartime engines of Packard," *Hemmings Classic Car,* January 2006, 46.

[195] Torrence, 47.

[196] "Packard's Plans," *Business Week,* 12 August, 1944, 75-76.

[197] "Autos get ready," Business Week, 26 February, 1944, 21.

[198] Gunnell, 523-524.

[199] Hounshell, 125.

[200] Gunnell, 519-520.

[201] Donnelly, 49.

[202] Gunnell, 533.

Chapter 10

Democratization of Luxury
1927-1965

Cadillac pursued a path in its advertising starting well before World War II that opened new markets for its products. The cars were portrayed as luxuries that anyone could eventually own, if only they worked hard. Many consumer goods found in modern households were once considered luxuries. Refrigerators, radios, televisions, telephones and automobiles all began as curiosities for the wealthy. Over the ensuing decades, they have become almost universal. The shortages of World War Two forced consumers to consider the products that they wished to purchase when the war ended. According to an article in a September 1943 issue of the *New York Daily News*, soldiers believed that they were fighting for the right to buy a variety of products after the war including cuffed pants, steak, and new golf balls.[203] These could all be termed luxury items. Cuffs on pants, while very stylish, serve no real function. Steak and hamburger come from the same source. Golf is a leisure activity once reserved for the wealthy. The fact that servicemen were thinking about post war purchasing of non-essential items during wartime implies a possible trend that manufacturers could exploit. The post war world would likely welcome the democratized luxury consumer.

Applied to automobiles, this idea holds that consumers will gradually demand greater quality and more amenities in their cars. The Model T was wonderful for the market of 1910. However, by 1946, people wanted finely upholstered seats, heaters, radios, and automatic transmissions in their cars. It does not take a marketing genius to conclude that the company that could produce an automobile with these features at a reasonable price would do well in the post war market. Cadillac's Series 60 Special had successfully applied this to automobiles in the late 1930s. Packard and Lincoln failed to democratized luxury to the extent that Cadillac had. Their personal luxury cars were simply too exclusive for a large audience. After the war, Packard went to the other extreme and brought the Packard down to the middle price level for good, sacrificing prestige for sales.

Cadillac as Icon: 1928-1965

In the late 1930s, Cadillac was in the process of changing the image of the luxury car from a chauffer driven status symbol to a sporty, fun to drive machine. In the 1920s and early 1930s, Cadillacs and the companion LaSalles were portrayed in print ads as exclusive machines of the wealthy. In "L'Opera: LaSalle- Car of those who lead," the 1928 LaSalle was pictured in front of a regal theatre. The car was surrounded by men in top hats and tails. The owner of the LaSalle is visible in the back seat. His chauffer is mostly obscured behind the windshield post, but the reader can readily recognize his position.[204] A 1933 ad for a Cadillac V-12 open front town car showed finely dressed men and women enjoying a very formal party. The after discussing the mechanical superiority of the car, the ad copy mentions that, "it is because of these things that Cadillac has come to occupy the unchallenged position it does among America's first families...."[205] Clearly, these cars were not aimed at the masses. Most Americans did not go to the opera in 1928, nor did they have chauffeurs who drove town cars for them in

1933. It would be a few years before the driver/owner moved to the forefront of Cadillac advertising.

By the late 1930s, the driver/owner had emerged as a primary character in Cadillac ads. "America's most <u>imitated</u> motor car" showed the new 1938 Series 60 Special whizzing by an ultramodern industrial building. The driver, fedora atop his crown, was speeding along in the company of four women, most likely his immediate family. The copy noted that "No other car approaches it for performance, comfort, vision, or handling ease."[206] The owner of a chauffer driven luxury car would have little care for these issues. He was merely a passenger, rather than an active participant, in his travels.

There were some ads than straddled the traditional and personal luxury fields. The Series 72 was offered for only one season, 1940. The ad, "Presenting a new Cadillac-Fleetwood at a much lower price!" presented a familiar picture to the public. The sedan was parked at the entrance of a grand hotel, with a chauffer at his proper station behind the wheel. Interestingly, the idea of the owner/driver appears in this otherwise conventional ad.

> It is equally suited for chauffeur or owner driving. In fact, it is so nimble and quick to handle that it is highly suited to individual transportation. For the family that wants an all-purpose car- equally proper for the formal occasion or for general usage- the new Cadillac-Fleetwood Seventy-Two is without a rival.[207]

The copy writer might have overstated his case, as the locomotive-esque Series 72 was nimble only when compared to the Rock of Gibraltar. Nevertheless, the point that this fine luxury car was not reserved only for the super-rich would not have been lost on the reader. While ads like this were much more rare before World War II than after, it is clear that Cadillac was moving in the direction of democratizing luxury.

Print advertising was vital during World War II as a means of keeping Cadillac buyers interested in the product. After the war ended, advertising sold the idea that Cadillac was the unquestioned leader of the luxury field, even if production numbers did not necessarily show that. Only in 1946 and 1947 was there any reference to the war, with the latter's sole clue to the wartime past a large "V" in the background of the ad. The former, 1946's "Cadillac-improved even more in war than in peace!" told the story of the V-8/Hydra-Matic combo being used in tanks during World War II.[208] Any mention of the company's wartime activities were henceforth confined to the styling of the cars. For the most part, ads of the time proclaimed the theme that the owner and driver of the modern luxury car were one and the same. Additionally, the Cadillac was presented as a symbol of excellence and prestige, the key to an upper class world that was open to an increasing number of people after the war.

As the 1950s began, the idea that a Cadillac was far more affordable than its reputation might suggest was promoted. "Wanted... by almost half the people!" appeared in *Holiday* in November 1950. A red 1950 Fleetwood Series 60 Special was set against a green background. A fine ruby and diamond necklace by Van Cleef and Arpels flanked a large Cadillac crest above the car. Such jewelry was available only to the well-to-do elites, so the implication that Cadillac was a prestigious automobile would not have been missed. The copy noted that when asked to choose the most desirable automobile in America, consumers chose the Cadillac by a margin of five to one over the nearest competitor. Owning such a fine car was not out of reach for many of these people. "Cadillac's relatively modest price, its unusual operating economy and long life, make it a far more practical and sensible possession than many motorists realize."[209] Those who could afford to give their wives ruby necklaces owned Cadillacs, but those of more limited means could do the same. Luxury was not only prestigious, but it was also a logical choice.

Cadillacs were not only affordable and practical luxury that was enjoyable to drive, but they also improved the disposition of the men who drove them. "Cadillac- Brings out the best in a man!" featured a blue 1955 Fleetwood Series 60 Special in the lower third of the ad. The main focus was a man having a bust sculpted. Obviously, he was a man of wealth and power, as few commoners need to have their busts molded by professionals. The reader learns that the fellow in the chair, while much more powerful than most people, was not immune to the charm of a new Cadillac.

> Wonderful things happen to a man when he takes the wheel of his Cadillac. To begin with, he looks his best! There's a pride in his face..and happiness in his heart...and confidence in his bearing... as he sits in command of the "car of cars." And how grand he feels! The car carries him in perfect comfort...and there is so little effort to his driving that he completely relaxes as he rides. And even his character takes on new graciousness- pausing to allow pedestrians to make their way...and offering every courtesy and consideration to his fellow motorists. All this is to say, of course, that a Cadillac brings out the very best in a man. In fact, owners everywhere freely admit that the car acts as a wonderful tonic for their spirit and outlook and disposition. And of course, the Cadillac car for 1955 offers more of everything to delight its lucky owners...and to inspire their contentment and satisfaction. Incidentally, this is the perfect time to make the move to Cadillac...from a standpoint of both economy and delivery. Why not visit your Cadillac dealer soon and see for yourself?[210]

It is clear from this ad that a true luxury car such as Cadillac not only makes others think that the owner is an important person, but it actually improves the driver's personality.

The 1960s brought a new emphasis on youth. The 1965 DeVille convertible was billed as a sports car in "Some people like the sports cars big and luxurious." The pleasure of driving the car was coupled with the high level of luxury available.

> That's why the new 1965 Cadillac is their car. For here is an automobile with all the action that anyone could ask for- and all the size and comfort as well. Its big high performance engine is truly dynamic- and its Turbo Hydra-Matic transmission is smooth and quiet as never before. And this newest of Cadillacs

is more agile than ever in its handling. With new frame and suspension design and a wider tread, the 1965 Cadillac holds the road better than many a car that flashes a rally stripe. Try motoring's richest and most exciting combination of size, comfort and luxury- and action. It's waiting for you now.[211]

This ad perfectly embodies the personal luxury principle laid out by the Series 60 Special in 1938 and extolled in 1939's "500 Miles- and still an hour to sunset."[212] A luxury car had to be large, powerful, and prestigious. At the same time, it had to be a joy to drive. This concept was born in the late 1930s, grew technologically through World War II, and matured in the 1950s. By the mid-1960s, the democratization of the luxury automobile was complete.

Chapter 10 Notes

[203] Cohen, 73.

[204] Cadillac Motor Car Division, "L'Opera: LaSalle- Car of those who lead," *The Self Starter*, March 2002, 30.

[205] Cadillac Motor Car Division, "Cadillac- A General Motors value," *The Self Starter*, November-December, 1996, front cover.

[206] Cadillac Motor Car Division, "America's most imitated motor car!" *The Self Starter*, May 2002, 30.

[207] Cadillac Motor Car Division, "Presenting a new Cadillac-Fleetwood at a much lower price!" magazine advertisement, 1940, in J.D. Shively Cadillac Literature Collection, Greencastle, Indiana.

[208] Cadillac Motor Car Division, "Cadillac-improved even more in war than in peace!" magazine advertisement, 1946, in J.D. Shively Cadillac Literature Collection, Greencastle, Indiana.

[209] Cadillac Motor Car Division, "Wanted... by almost half the people!" magazine advertisement, 1950, in J.D. Shively Cadillac Literature Collection, Greencastle, Indiana.

[210] Cadillac Motor Car Division, "Cadillac- Brings out the best in a man!" magazine advertisement, 1955, in J.D. Shively Cadillac Literature Collection, Greencastle, Indiana.

[211] Cadillac Motor Car Division, "Some people like the sports cars big and luxurious," magazine advertisement, 1965, in J.D. Shively Cadillac Literature Collection, Greencastle, Indiana.

[212] Prescott, 12.

Chapter 11

Cadillac Victorious!
1946-1949

The Second World War had been kind to Cadillac. The money the company saved on retooling allowed for more production options than rival companies could offer. The Clark Avenue plant saw many improvements during the war that allowed Cadillac to provide such an improved product so quickly. Most of the changes made for war production were easily adaptable for civilian use. An overhead conveyer system was installed in 1944 for moving freshly cast engine blocks from the foundry to the machine shop more efficiently. Cadillac Engineering got new dynamometer rooms outfitted with the latest technology, something that would come in handy when testing new engines. The foundry was modernized. Many of the well-trained wartime employees wanted to stay at Cadillac after the war, reducing time and capital losses to retraining. With driveline production in fantastic shape, all that was needed was to remove the 1942 body dies from storage and start making cars.[213] Were it not for things that Cadillac could not control, such as labor unrest and steel shortages, it is quite possible that 1946 production would have rivaled 1941's numbers.

New for '46

The first post war car, a 1946 Ford, rolled off the line in October, 1945. Cadillac followed shortly after, with the first new Packards not arriving until November. The high hopes of many companies for post war production were soon dashed by strikes. On New Years Day 1946, only the Ford and Hudson plants were operational. Total production for 1945 was 85,786, with an additional 2,255,921 units the following calendar year.[214] Considering the steel shortages and an uncooperative U.A.W., this total was quite respectable.

The first new Cadillac in nearly four years, a 1946 Series 62 sedan, was completed on October 17, 1945. Thanks in great part to the obstinacy of the U.A.W., no other model was available until the following April. Despite this difficulty and a severe cold-rolled steel shortage, Cadillac managed to produce nearly 30,000 cars during the 1946 model year.[215] Packard outsold its rival by less than 500 units, including Junior models, but Cadillac was well on its way to becoming the dominant luxury make.

To the untrained eye, the 1946 Cadillac was little more than a warmed over 1942 model. A few cosmetic changes were made to the exterior trim to modernize the styling. Cadillac engineers had dismantled a well traveled 1942 sedan and noted trouble spots. Many mechanical improvements were derived from the military application 346 and Hydra-Matic combination. Durex 300 rod bearings were installed in the engine. Steel backing over a copper core provided longer wear. Three ring pistons were now standard. Valve guides were ferrox-treated for greater durability. Synthetic rubber water pump and generator belts promised greater intervals between changes. The transmission also received upgrades. A hydraulic blocking valve was installed to keep the forward gears from engaging while the selector was in reverse, resulting in less clashing during shifting. The rear planetary gear was redesigned, as were the front and rear bands. A new oil pump distributed fluid more efficiently. The fin spacing inside the torus was changed, providing for more silent operation.[216] All of these changes combined to give Cadillac a much improved product for its dealers to sell to an eager public.

Cadillac buyers could choose from two distinctive types of cars in the early post war era. Those who wanted prestige could still buy the Fleetwood Series 75, complete with blind rear quarters and a divider window if so ordered. Buyers who wanted a high level of luxury while having the pleasure of driving their own cars chose the Fleetwood Series 60 Special or the more modestly priced luxury of the Series 61 and 62. Packard owners didn't have the same choices. The high priced and luxurious Senior cars were gone. The Clipper body was lengthened or shortened to meet the needs of the company, but the public was not convinced. By trying to be a middle-priced car with luxury overtones, Packard failed to fully satisfy either market.[217] Although it outsold Cadillac in sheer volume in 1946, 1948, and 1949, the post war Packard simply wasn't the same car that it was before the war. Cadillac was now clearly setting the standard in the luxury car world.

Harley Earl, founder and director of General Motors' Division of Art and Colour, had a long standing love affair with aviation. He appreciated the practical application of streamlining. Knowing this, stylist Bill Mitchell sometimes included aircraft in his sketches during the late 1930s and early 1940s.[218] Mr. Earl knew the commanding officer at Selfridge Field in Michigan, so he gained permission for his styling staff to visit the base and see the new Lockheed P-38 Lightning in early 1941. The fighter's twin booms, with their streamlined cowls and sleek rudders, inspired the designers. Franklin Q. Hershey, a veteran of Walter M. Murphy Company's design studio, was hired by Earl to work on an advanced design based on the P-38 that was dubbed the "Interceptor Series." This project was put on hold until late 1944, when Hershey returned from the military. No expenses were spared on the project, so the most skilled stylists were hired to help with the Interceptor. The strikes of the early post war era didn't deter this hardy band, who often took refuge in the basement of Hershey's farmhouse north of Detroit. Most of the designs that they created were impractically streamlined, with bubble canopies and sharply pointed prows. By June 1946, the final form of the first entirely new post war Cadillac, the 1948 model, had taken shape.[219]

Fishtailed '48s

The 1948 Cadillac looked like nothing else on the road when it entered showrooms on February 4, 1948. An integrated three tiered look emerged. The first tier bore more than a passing resemblance to the P-38's twin booms. The headlights mimicked propeller hubs. The remainder of the front fender, front door, and half of the rear door followed the line of the boom. The rear door and rear fender bulged out, much as the air intakes on the P-38. The rear fender culminated in a small tailfin that doubled as a taillight.[220] The car resembled the P-38 when viewed from above. The headlights resembled the tips of the propeller hubs, while the point of the hood represented the nose of the Lockheed fighter.[221] The aircraft styling was carried over to the interior. Instead of being a series of three round clusters, as had been the case from 1942-1947, the instruments were arranged in a single pod, the shape of which resembled the instrument panel of an aircraft.[222]

Aircraft Styling

It is quite understandable why Cadillac would choose an aircraft theme for its post war car designs. During the war, the company had often bragged about the fighters for which it produced engine parts. The M-5 and M-24 were entirely Cadillac built products, but olive drab armor plate simply wasn't as glamorous as the sleek polished aluminum skin of a warbird. Interestingly, this aviation theme would continue for fifty years. The tailfins became much longer, taller and sharper, culminating in the forty three inch fins of 1959. By 1965 the fins were gone, but the aviation theme continued. The taillights had been grouped into two widely spaced pods starting in 1957. All Fleetwoods carried this rear end motif until the line was discontinued in 1996. The deVille series kept it three years longer, losing this identity during the 2000 restyle. Jet age styling affected the front of the cars for many years, at least through 1964.[223] If one looks at the front bumper pods of a 1960 Cadillac, the resemblance to one of a B-52's engine fairings is quite striking.[224] The "goddess of speed" hood ornament became more streamlined with each passing year. By its last season, 1956, the goddess resembled a jet plane more than the mythical woman. Inside the cars, the aviation theme reappeared numerous times over the next few decades, particularly in the instrument panel.[225]

Overhead valves for Cadillac- 1949

While Cadillac was making strides in styling, engineering was not being neglected. A new engine design was commissioned in the late 1930s under the direction of Harry F. Barr. Future Cadillac president John F. Gordon spent time on the project in the early 1940s. After World War II ended, Ed Cole's work as chief engineer began in earnest. The lessons learned from tank production were applied to the new engine. Internal parts were made even more durable than in the flathead engine. The new engine was ready for the beginning of the 1949 model year. Unlike its predecessor, it was an overhead valve design. Piston specialist Byron Ellis created slipper pistons for the engine. The lower sides of the pistons were cut away, allowing them to nestle between the crankshaft counterweights at the bottom of the stroke. This permitted a longer stoke inside a smaller engine block. The new engine displaced 331 cubic inches and produced 160 sixty horsepower. Despite this improvement, it weighed 188 pounds less than the 1948 engine and was four inches lower and shorter than its predecessor.[226] This improved engine was utilized with minimal modifications until 1962, when a new block was introduced for the 1963 model year.[227] The general overhead valve design was used by Cadillac until the advent of the Northstar dual overhead cam engine, which debuted in the 1993 model year. Ed Cole left Cadillac for Chevrolet, taking his 331 V-8 design with him. Mr. Cole's engine first rested in a Chevy engine bay in 1955. With some modifications, this same engine is still used by full size GMC and Chevrolet trucks five decades later. Although Packard outsold Cadillac in 1949, the handwriting was on the wall. The overhead valve engine, coupled with a modest facelift on the 1948 restyle, gave Cadillac the knockout punch that it needed to finally defeat Packard. Jack Bond, of *Motor Trend*, liked the 1949 Cadillac so much that he named it "Car of the Year," the first such honor bestowed by the magazine.[228]

Concluding thoughts

Cadillac's definition of luxury that originated in the 1930s still holds true today. The car must provide prestige as well as power, making it an appropriate choice for the highways or an afternoon at the country club. It must be a joy to drive, placing the owner/driver in a better state of mind. To aid in this, it need not be outrageously priced, but it had to be built with a quality that would appear to exceed the sticker price. All of these parameters were set by Cadillac thanks to its engineers and ad writers during the 1940s, 1950s, and 1960s.

Cadillac has been the premier luxury car during the post war era thanks to seeds that were sown over a century ago. Henry M. Leland's obsession with precision created an environment for excellence that engineers today still practice on every new Cadillac that they design. The company has always striven to be innovative, from the first self starter to the modern Northstar system. Both world wars allowed Cadillac to demonstrate how well its products held up under the most adverse conditions. The Second World War was more important in that the company continued to improve its products and production facilities at War Department expense. Packard, Cadillac's primary rival during the first half of the twentieth century, did not have this advantage and was forced to spend vast sums of money to resume civilian production. Most importantly, Cadillac was able to redefine what luxury meant, and to be that definition. In 1930, Cadillac raised the technological bar by introducing the world's first V-16 automobile engine. After its competitors exhausted their resources trying to compete with the V-16, Cadillac changed the rules again. By the 1940s, cars had to be owner driven, easy to maintain, and stylish to be considered luxury cars. This theme continued after World War II to the present day in the guise of the Eldorado, Seville, and the CTS. Finally, Cadillac defined luxury as something within the reach of the masses. With a little luck, hard work, and persistence, any American could own a Cadillac someday. Cadillac became the leader of the fine car field by setting the standards, rather than following the lead of others. If the company continues on this path, Cadillac will remain the "Standard of the World" in the twenty first century.

Chapter 11 Notes

[213] Schneider, *Cadillacs of the Forties*, 93.

[214] Kimes, 667.

[215] Schneider, *Cadillacs of the Forties*, 93.

[216] "Announcing the New Cadillac for 1946," *Cadillac Serviceman*, November 1945, 40-41.

[217] Prescott, 11-13.

[218] Schneider, *Cadillacs of the Forties*, 74.

[219] Schneider, *Cadillacs of the Forties*, 123-124.

[220] Ibid., 128-129.

[221] Roy Schneider, "Cadillac's final triumph of the Forties," *The Self Starter*, June 1999, 11.

[222] Ibid., 133.

[223] Roy A. Schneider, *Cadillacs of the Sixties* (Temple City, California: Cadillac Motorbooks, 1995), 83.

[224] Cadillac Motor Car Division, *1960 Cadillac Sales Training Film*, Produced by General Motors Corporation. 1959. 30 min. filmstrip.

[225] Cadillac Motor Car Division, *1960 Cadillac Options Specifications Manual,* (Detroit, Michigan: Sales Distribution Department, Cadillac Motor Car Division, 1959), 32.

Cadillac Motor Car Division, *Cadillac Style- 1992* (Detroit, Michigan: General Motors Corporation, 1991), 4-5.

Cadillac Motor Car Division, *2003 Cadillac* (Detroit, Michigan: General Motors Corporation, 2002), 4.

[226] McCall, 279.

[227] Schneider, *Cadillacs of the Sixties*, 72.

[228] Schneider, "Cadillac's final triumph of the Forties," 10.

Appendix A
Cadillac/LaSalle and Packard Production
1929-1942

Year/make	Cadillac 8	Cadillac 12	Cadillac 16	LaSalle	Packard 6 110 or 115	Packard8 Light 8 or 120	Packard 8 Standard Deluxe	Packard Twin 6
1929	18103	0	0	22961	0	0	55081	0
1930	14995	0	2887	11005	0	0	3693	0
1931	10717	5733	364	10103	0	0	3345	0
1932	2700	1740	300	3290	0	6785	9326	583
1933	2100	953	126	3381	0	0	4336	547
1934	8318	1098	150	7218	0	0	9093	986
1935	'34+'35	'34+'35	'34+'35	8653	0	25175	6839	856
1936	11960	901	52	13004	0	55136	5361	718
1937	11235	478	50	32005	65603	50266	7175	1300
1938	9143	0	315	15501	30159	22700	2476	569
1939	13495	0	138	23028	24350	19536	6022	496
1940	12984	0	51 (10)	24133	62610	28319	10646	0
1941	66169	0	0	0	34700	17100	21879	0
1942	16513	0	0	0	11325	19199	3252	0

Data from *The Classic Era*, www.parkardclub.org, *Standard Catalog of Cadillac: 1903-1990*.

Appendix B
Luxury Car Production
1946-1965

Year/make	Cadillac	LaSalle	Continental	Imperial	Lincoln	Packard
1946	29194	0	0	750	17111	30793
1947	61926	0	0	for	21460	51086
1948	50640	0	0	1946-48	7769	80012
1949	92554	0	0	135	73507	112928
1950	86590	0	0	11,064	28154	46650
1951	110340	0	0	27,698	20295	100322
1952	90259	0	0	'51-52	27271	69601
1953	109651	0	0	9018	40762	86059
1954	96680	0	0	5758	36993	33672
1955	140777	0	0	11430	27222	55517
1956	155577	0	2550	10628	50322	28835
1957	124233	0	446	37593	41123	4809
1958	121778	0	11550	16233	17134	2622
1959	142272	0	11126	17269	15780	0
1960	142184	0	11086	17719	13734	0
1961	138274	0	0	12258	25160	0
1962	160840	0	0	14337	31061	0
1963	180064	0	0	14121	31233	0
1964	165847	0	0	23295	36297	0
1965	181435	0	0	18409	40380	0

Data: *Standard Catalog of American Cars: 1946-1975.*

Bibliography

PrimaryDocuments
Manuals and In House Publications

Cadillac Motor Car Company. *Cadillac Participation in the World War*. Detroit, Michigan: Cadillac Motor Car Company, 1919.

Cadillac Motor Car Division. *Cadillac Air Conditioning Manual*. Detroit, Michigan: Service Department, Cadillac Motor Car Division, 1941.

Cadillac Motor Car Division. *Cadillac and Cadillac Fleetwood for 1941*. Detroit, Michigan: Service Department, Cadillac Motor Car Division, 1940.

Cadillac Motor Car Division. *Cadillac and Cadillac Fleetwood for 1942*. Detroit, Michigan: Service Department, Cadillac Motor Car Division, 1941.

Cadillac Motor Car Division. *Cadillac...From Peace to War*. Detroit, Michigan: Service Department, Cadillac Motor Car Division, 1944.

Cadillac Motor Car Division. *Cadillac Shop Manual for 1942*. Detroit, Michigan: Service Department, Cadillac Motor Car Division, 1941.

Cadillac Motor Car Division. *Cadillac Style-1992*. Detroit, Michigan: General Motors Corporation, 1991.

Cadillac Motor Car Division. *Operating Hints for the 1941 Cadillac*. Detroit, Michigan: General Motors Sales Corporation, 1940.

Cadillac Motor Car Division. *1941 Cadillac Salesman's Databook*. Detroit, Michigan: General Motors Sales Corporation, September 17, 1940.

Cadillac Motor Car Division. *1960 Cadillac Options Specifications Manual*. Detroit, Michigan: Sales Distribution Department, Cadillac Motor Car Division, 1959.

Cadillac Motor Car Division.*1960 Cadillac Sales Training Film*. Produced by General Motors Corporation. 1959. 30 min. filmstrip.

Cadillac Motor Car Division. *Seville 2000*. General Motors Corporation, Detroit, Michigan, 2000.

Cadillac Motor Car Division. *2002 Seville*. Detroit, Michigan: General Motors Corporation, 2002.

Cadillac Motor Car Division. *2003 Cadillac*. Detroit, Michigan: General Motors Corporation, 2002.

Customer Research Staff, General Motors Corporation. *The Automobile User's Guide with Wartime Suggestions*. Detroit, Michigan: General Motors Corporation, 1944.

Sherwin Williams Automotive Finishes. "1941 Cadillac Passenger Car Production Colors."

Cadillac In House Periodicals

"Actual Need Only Sound Basis for Parts Sales." *Cadillac Serviceman*, March-April 1942, 8.

"Announcing the New Cadillac for 1946." *Cadillac Serviceman*. November 1945, 40-41.

"Break a Tool, Jap's Delight." *Cadillac Serviceman*. September-October 1942, 22.

"Cadillac Mileage Extension Plan." *Cadillac Serviceman*. March-April 1942, 7,9.

"Cadillac Servicemen Play an Important Role in Maintaining Owner Goodwill at High Level." *Cadillac Serviceman*. November-December 1943, 21.

"Cadillac Victory Sweepstakes." *Cadillac Serviceman*. September-October 1943, 17-18.

"Lower Octane Fuels." *Cadillac Serviceman*. January-February 1942, 6.

"Most Cadillac Accessories Still Available at Factory." *Cadillac Serviceman*. July-August 1942, 18.

"Newly Developed Cadillac Wheel Locks Prevent Theft of Tires and Wheels." *Cadillac Serviceman*. July-August 1942, 12.

"Proper Procedure for storage of new cars is required to provide maximum protection." *Cadillac Serviceman*. March-April 1942, 9, 11.

"Scrap is Ammunition." *Cadillac Serviceman*. January-February 1943, 2.

"Steel needed." *Cadillac Serviceman*. July-August 1943, 14.

"Thorough Inspection is keynote to longer car life." *Cadillac Serviceman*. July-August 1942, 17-18.

"W.P.B. Announces New Drive to Build Scrap Reserve." *Cadillac Serviceman*. September-October 1943, 19.

"1942 Service Price Book Now Meets OPA Regulations." *Cadillac Serviceman*. July-August 1942, 20.

Other Periodicals

"Auto Shutdown?" *Business Week*. 7 December 1941, 19.

"Auto trim change." *Business Week*. 29 November 1941, 17-18.

"Autos get ready." Business Week. 26 February 1944, 21.

"Autos to Tanks." *Business Week*. 15 November 1941, 17-18.

"Back to war job: renewed demand for tanks." *Business Week*. 8 July, 1944, 22-23.

"Car-less Dealers?" *Business Week*. 7 December 1941, 20.

"Cars on the skids." *Business Week*. 27 June 1942, 64.

Ethridge, John. "GM's Crown Jewel." Motor Trend. August 1965, 38-41.

"First Cast Steel Tank. *Business Week*. 7 December 1941, 17.

"GM Defense Job: armament program's impact on American Industry." *Business Week.* 14 December 1940, 28.

"GM War Service Program." *Aviation.* May 1942, 190.

Gordon, John F. Chief Engineer, Cadillac Motor Car Division. "Cadillac Twin V-8 Power Plant for Light Tanks." reprinted in *The Self Starter.* Fall 1992, 9-15.

"Heavy Tank Armor." *Business Week.* 18 October 1941, 18-19.

"How industry is training war mechanics." *Newsweek.* 23 November 1942, 54.

"M3: The army's newest tank." *Time.* 14 April 1941, 22-23.

"Memo to a post-war planner." *Business Week.* 14 June 1941, 84.

New Jersey Zinc Company "Zinc in Defense" Business Week. 29 November 1941, 9.

"No'Bright Work." *Business Week.* 1 November 1941, 16-17.

"Packard's Plans." *Business Week.* 12 August 1944, 75-76.

"Recooked Autos?" *Business Week.* 25 October 1941, 67.

"Repair is stressed in new tank program." *Business Week.* 22 July 1944, 47.

"Retreader's Boom." *Business Week.* 7 December 1941, 26.

"Tanks: Coming up." *Business Week.* 17 May 1941, 22.

Texaco Corporation. "Wanted...more miracles!" *Business Week.* 19 January 1946, 3.

"Training speeded: military need for repair and maintenance specialists spurs GM output to over 2000 trainees a month." *Business Week.* 16 January 1943.

"V-8 for victory: Ford engine for medium tanks as army's choice." *Business Week.* 19 December 1942, 14.

Primary Sources
Films

Cadillac Motor Car Division. *1960 Cadillac Sales Training Film.* Produced by General Motors Corporation. 1959. 30 min. filmstrip.

John Huston. The War Department. *Report from the Aleutians.* 1944. 60 min. motion picture.

Secondary Sources
Books

Angelucci, Enzo. *The Rand McNally Encyclopedia of Military Aircraft, 1914-1980.* New York: The Military Press, 1977, 233-234.

Automobile Manufacturers Association. *Freedom's Arsenal: the story of the Automotive Council for War Production.* Detroit: The Automobile Manufacturers Association, 1950.

Cohen, Lizabeth. *A Consumers' Republic: The Politics of Mass Consumption in Postwar America. Vintage Books: New York, 2003.*

Gunnell, John. ed. *Standard Catalog of American Cars: 1946-1975.* Iola, Wisconsin: Krause Publications, 1991.

Hendry, Maurice D. *Cadillac: Standard of the World: The Complete 70 Year History.* Princeton, New Jersey: Princeton Publishing,1973.

Kimes, Beverly Rae. *The Classic Era.* Des Plaines, Illinois: Classic Car Club of America, 2001.

Kennett, Lee. *For the Duration: The United States Goes to War, Pearl Harbor-1942.* New York: Charles Scribner's Sons, 1985.

Kuhn, Arthur J. *GM passes Ford, 1918-1938: designing the General Motors performance-control system.* University Park: Pennsylvania State University Press, 1986.

Leland, Winifred C. *Master of Precision: Henry M. Leland.* Detroit, MI: Wayne State University Press, 1966.

Malks, Josh B. *Cord 810/812 :The Timeless Classic.* Iola, Wisconsin: Krause Publications, 1995.

McCall, Walter M.P. *Eighty Years of Cadillac LaSalle.* Osceola, Wisconsin: Motorbooks International Publishers, 1982.

Nineteen Forty-One Authenticity Team. *Authenticity Manual, Class 11- 1941 Cadillac.* Columbus, Ohio: Cadillac-LaSalle Club, Inc., 2004.

Pound, Arthur. *The turning wheel; the story of General Motors through twenty-five years, 1908-1933.*Garden City, New York: Doubleday, Doran and Company, Inc., 1934.

Schneider, Roy A. *Cadillacs of the Forties*. Temple City, California: Cadillac Motorbooks, 1999.

Schneider, Roy A. *Cadillacs of the Sixties*. Temple City, California: Cadillac Motorbooks, 1995.

Sieber, Mary and Ken Buttolph, ed. *Standard Catalog of Cadillac: 1903-1990*. Iola, Wisconsin: Krause Publications, 1991.

Sivulka, Juliann. *Soap, Sex, and Cigarettes: A Cultural History of American Advertising*. Wadsworth Publishing Agency: Belmont, CA, 1998.

Van Gelderen, Ron and Matt Larson. *LaSalle: Cadillac's Companion Car*. Paducah, Kentucky: Turner Publishing, 2000.

Periodicals

Ayres, Paul. "The Demise of the Cadillac Clark Avenue Plant:1921-1995." *The Classic Car*. March 1999, 46-48.

Brockman, Eric. "One Man's Art: Rudolf Bauer and the last Duesenberg." *Cars and Parts*. July 1995, 20-26,62.

Brown, Arch. "Black Beauty: 1941 Lincoln Continental Coupe." *Cars and Parts*. January 1998, 52-58.

Brown, Arch. "Cadillac- A Complete History, Part VIII: In wartime and beyond." *Cars and Parts*. August 1991, 40-43.

Crabtree, Jim. "Conspicuous Consumption and Classic Cars." *The Classic Car*. December 1998, 18-19.

Davis, Darrell. "The First Eight-Cylinder Chrysler Imperials." *The Classic Car*. Summer 2005, 26.

Donnelly, Jim. "Powering to victory: The revolutionary wartime engines of Packard." *Hemmings Classic Car*. January 2006, 46.

Hendry, Maurice D. "Comparing the Performance of Classic 'Muscle' Cars." *The Classic Car*. September 1999, 51.

Hoffman, Jack. "The High Output Cadillac Tank Engine Program," *The Self Starter*, October 1999, 18-20.

Houston, Doug. "The Role of Classic engines in World War II." *The Classic Car*, July 2005, 18-19

Kaminsky, Eric. "1931 Marmon V-16 Coupe." *Cars and Parts*. February 2003, 16-21.

Langworth, Richard M. "The Packard Darrins: Immortal creations of a breakaway designer." *Collectable Automobile*. June 1992, 28-37.

Mueller, Mike."1927 Duesenberg Straight 8- The little-known Model X." *Cars and Parts*. July 2002, 23-33.

Orwig, George E.II, "Marmon: The Final Chapter," *Antique Automobile*, July-August 1997, 7-14.

Padgett, Nina. "1932 Duesenberg Torpedo: back home in Indiana." *Car Collector and Car Classics*. June 1993, 28-32.

Peterson, West. "1939 Lincoln Continental: One more notch for Edsel and Gregorie." *Cars and Parts*, March 2003, 10-15.

Peterson, West. "1946 Lincoln Continental Cabriolet: Being seen in a personal luxury automobile." *Cars and Parts*. March 2000, 32-36.

Prescott, Joel. "After the Ball." *The Classic Car*. December 2000, 11-13.

Richardson, Jim. "A Packard for the Proletariat." *Classic Auto Restorer*. June 1992,60-63.

Schneider, Roy. "Cadillac's final triumph of the Forties," *The Self Starter*, June 1999 10-11, 18.

Skinner, Phil. "The Town Car: Under the skin, it's still a Duesenberg." *Cars and Parts*. July 1997, 52-54.

Stanley, Richard. "What's so special about the 1938 Sixty Special? Part I." *The Self Starter* April 2003, 11-16.

Stanley, Richard. "What's so special about the 1938 Sixty Special? Part III." *The Self Starter* June 2003, 11-13, 21.

Stevens, Bob. "Bohman & Schwartz customizes a '40 Packard." *Cars and Parts*. February 1998, 44-49.

Torrence, Neil. "Did the Packard Win the War or Was It a Casualty Thereof?" *The Classic Car*. June 1999,48-49.

Wenger, Terry. "Survivor! the story of the 1938-1940 Cadillac V-16." *The Classic Car*. Autumn 2004, 7.

Wright, Nicky. "The Adventures of CUW109: The tale of a much-traveled Duesenberg." *Car Collector and Car Classics*. November 1980,36-40.

Collections

Cadillac-LaSalle Club Museum and Research Center, Inc. Detroit, Michigan. Tim Pawl, President.

J.D. Shively Cadillac Literature Collection. Greencastle, Indiana. Jeffrey Shively, owner.

Websites

1930s Packard Database. Packard Owners Club website; available from http://www.packardclub.org; Internet; accessed 30 May, 2005.

2000 BMW Production Figures; available from http://64.224.175.31/european_companies/BMW/bmwsales.htm; accessed 30 May, 2005.

2000 Cadillac Production Figures; available from http://64.224.175.31/nao_companies/general_motors/gmsales3.htm; accessed 30 May, 2005.

2000 Lexus Production Figures; available from http://64.224.175.31/asian_companies/toyota_motor/business/toyota-us-sales-2000-by-model.htm; accessed 30 May, 2005.

2000 Mercedes Benz Production Figures; available from http://64.224.175.31/nao_companies/daimlerchrysler/dc-business-figures/merc-pass-car-sales-01.htm; accessed 30 May, 2005.

73131575R00086

Made in the USA
Columbia, SC
05 July 2017